Almon Gunnison

Wayside and Fireside Rambles

Sketches, reminiscences, and confessions

Almon Gunnison

Wayside and Fireside Rambles
Sketches, reminiscences, and confessions

ISBN/EAN: 9783337256548

Printed in Europe, USA, Canada, Australia, Japan

Cover: Foto ©Andreas Hilbeck / pixelio.de

More available books at **www.hansebooks.com**

WAYSIDE AND FIRESIDE RAMBLES.

Sketches, Reminiscences, and Confessions.

BY

ALMON GUNNISON,

AUTHOR OF "RAMBLES OVERLAND."

WITH ILLUSTRATIONS BY FREDERICK REMINGTON
AND WILLIAM HAMILTON GIBSON.

BOSTON:
UNIVERSALIST PUBLISHING HOUSE.
1894.

Copyright, 1893,
By ALMON GUNNISON.

University Press:
JOHN WILSON AND SON, CAMBRIDGE, U.S.A.

PREFACE.

SOME of the sketches which are brought together to form this book were first published in the paper with which the author has been connected for several years. This fact will explain the use of the much-abused editorial "we," which will attract the attention and stir the wrath of the ever-esteemed critic. There are times when it is simply impossible to do without the comprehensive "we" as a covering for the nakedness of one's egotism, and it is to be hoped that the genial critic, recognizing a modesty of which he is perhaps personally ignorant, will excuse this conventional but comforting device. If the book seems to be somewhat personal, it will be noticed that among other things it professes to be a book of confessions. It has been written in the infrequent intervals of a busy life, and it makes no appeal to be considered as a classic. The author hopes, however, that it may give a little cheer to its readers, — should it have any.

A. G.

WORCESTER, December, 1893.

CONTENTS.

	PAGE
ORATOR JOHN	9
MAYBROOK FARM	21
THE HARVEST OF A QUIET EYE	36
THE HOUSE THAT PETE BUILT	50
OLD YEAR'S REVERIES	62
AN EVENING WITH THE NEGROES	72
RUNNING THE GAUNTLET OF THE "ISMS" . .	81
A SHATTERED DREAM	92
"WHITE WINGS"	101
SORRENTO	106
A LOST ART	112
THE SPRING CLEANING	122
A DREAM OF THE ADRIATIC	126
THE STORY OF A MOTHER	134
THE HEROES OF ONE SHOW	143
THE CONFESSIONS OF A BASHFUL MAN . . .	158

THE SHADOW SIDE	172
WITH THE RANK OF CAPTAIN	183
THE STUDENT'S WORKSHOP	190
THE PARSON'S SMALL BOY	200
AN ALASKAN VOYAGE	211
THE STOCKING AT THE CHIMNEY	220
THE LAST NIGHT IN THE OLD HOUSE	231

WAYSIDE AND FIRESIDE RAMBLES.

ORATOR JOHN.

AT the beginning of the fall term of '62 the Green Mountain Institute was at the zenith of its prosperity. Professor Saunders, who for several years had been at its post of control, had arrested the waning of its influence, and had brought it honorable repute. Students who had felt the mysterious charm which pervaded the little village, and the strange fascination of the young teacher's enthusiasm, had carried to their homes glowing reports of the school; and from the adjacent villages, and even from towns in States other than Vermont, young men and women in large numbers had come to pursue their studies in this country village.

Somewhere among the hills of New England, Nature may have hidden a more lovely village than South Woodstock, but one can wander far to find so nearly the ideal spot for the bright days of student life. A single street, lined with trim New England cottages; the white church with its open lawn; the old academy on the hill; the little river Kedron, bordered with trees and dark with shrubbery; the broad sweep of the shapely hills that rose on every side, — gave a grace and beauty to the little village, which, in spite of the more pretentious claims of its rivals of later years, has kept its fair pre-eminence.

Nowhere else did the forest paths seem to lead into such inviting depths of shade, nor the maples stand in such queenly pride. Not elsewhere was there such lustrous green of foliage; and in the autumn, when the early frosts touched the hills, and these old monarchs hung out their myriad banners in the hazy air, it seemed as if the atmosphere itself was bathed in color. Winter came early and lingered late, but there was wine in the air. The summer nights were things to be remembered; and a poet's land of dreams never rivalled in its enchantments the soft music of those Sabbath mornings, when far off upon the hills there came the sound of the church bells, broken into a thousand tones by the woods and hills.

Among the new students of the term was a long, lank young man from an adjoining village, whom we shall call John. He was large for his age, and of a confiding nature. By one of the strange accidents of school life he was sent to room with a young Massachusetts student, whose bump of fun was large, and who was by nature an inveterate tease. He soon found out that John was not without his weak points, and taking into his confidence one or two friends, a conspiracy was formed against the artless youth, which for several weeks afforded amusement to the school. A casual word revealed the fact that John made some pretentions to oratorical skill, and his ambition was inflamed by the most persistent flattery. In a few days he refused to go into the reading class, boldly asserting the professor's incompetency to instruct him. Knowing that by this disregard of rules he would be abandoned by the teacher to his fate, his flatterers proceeded to extravagant lengths.

It was the nightly entertainment of the little coterie of tormentors to assemble in one of the students' rooms, and there, prostrate on the floor, with ears close to the stove-pipe that came from the lower room, to listen to the elocutionary drill administered by the youthful orator to one of the number who, with the assumed interest of a disciple, sat for instruction at his feet. John was not an expert in pronunciation, and his renderings were not likely to escape the memory. "Parrhasius and the Captive" was one of his star pieces. With what vehemence he recited the lines, —

> "Parrhasius stood, gazing forgetfully
> Upon his canvas. There Prometheus lay
> Chained to the cold rocks of Mount Caucasus —
> The vulture at his vitals."

The light was not good, and the piece was new, and up the stove-pipe hole came the words, —

> "Pizarro stood, gazing forgetfully
> Upon his canvas. There Prometheus lay
> Chained to the cold rocks of Mount Caucasus —
> The vulture at his vittles."

With what assiduous care was John trained to speak, at the rhetorical exercises of Saturday, "The Maniac Mother;" with what extravagance of gesture, with what clawings of the air, did he shriek out the cries of the mad woman, while before him the students sat clutching the seats in their agonizing struggles to keep from explosive laughter. The performance over, the conspirators would vie with each other in their flatteries. "Never did Demosthenes stir men's hearts as had our John. Eloquence had found its greatest master in the pride of our school, and the future had its highest prizes waiting for the brow of this prodigy." Looking back, it seems incredible that human credulity could be so imposed upon. But it was so irresistibly funny; even the most stolid of students so entered into the humor of the thing; there was such unity of purpose and similarity of flattery on the part of his companions, — that even a wiser person than an overgrown country boy of sixteen might have been deluded. Interest in ordinary studies flagged. John had tasted the sweets of success; he had a mission in the world, and, encouraged by these friends, who were so deferential, who with such unanimity praised his talents and predicted his fame, day and night were spent in training for his oratorical displays.

The literary society met on Friday evenings. It was the social event of the week. The work in hand now was to bring the young orator out in debate. His past success had not been in the way of extemporaneous oratory, and even his monumental assurance shrank from the new ordeal. But patient pleadings prevailed, and the young man promised to appear if two of the confederates, "Bragg" and "Smith," would write his speech. The conditions were accepted and the work was done. For several weeks John was withdrawn from observation and carefully coached. Every possible extravagance of voice and gesture was impressed upon him; and when ingenuity could add no new absurdity, notice was given of the approaching exhibition.

The night came, and every seat in the Institute was crowded. Expectancy was at its height as John entered with his trainers. Art had been busy with the decoration of his person. His neck-tie was of flaring colors and huge proportions; his ample boots were brilliant with immaculate polish; his hair was beaded with the barber's oil; and as with an orator's art he drew his handkerchief, the air was filled with its heavy perfume. At the appointed time in the debate, John arose and delivered himself of the following, which we transcribe from a copy printed from the original notes. The question for debate was, "Resolved, that the traffic in intoxicating liquors should be suppressed by force." Our memory does not serve as to the side that John took, and the internal evidences of the speech unfortunately give little clew; but here are his words: —

"Ladies, Gentlemen, and Mr. President, — This question is one which concerns us all, individually, collectively, and emphatically. It is a subject that since the establishment of the Christian era, yea, ever since our forefathers, whose tracks of blood might be seen upon the desert sands of Cape Horn, landed upon the verdant rock of Plymouth, — ever since then, Mr. President, this subject has agitated the minds of all profound philosophers, statesmen, and tavern-keepers.

"It was for taking the opinion which I advocate here to-night, sir, that Socrates, that able general, that profound scholar and Christian man, met his fate gloriously upon the gallows. It was for taking this opinion that Demosthenes, that insatiate orator, but alas, confirmed drunkard, was executed by order of the British Government. But, Mr. President, I care not for their fate. I stand here to-night, in all the strength of my growing fame and powerful ability, to assert with a mighty voice the rights of man. Let no one charge me with dishonor, for I must, like the mountain eagle of the Andes, have my unrestrained liberty and freedom of speech. I can truly say in the language of the late Mr. Shakespeare (who, I am sorry to learn, recently met with an untimely end), 'Give me liberty or give me death.' I shall assert my opinion here to-night, Mr. President, on the floor of this house, freely, ignoramously, and idiotically. Sir, who, I ask, was he that carried the 'Star Spangled Banner' of France into the cold desert sands of Siberia, burned the Turkish Capitol, and led back his army amidst the vine-clad rocks and citron groves of sunny France? It was Napoleon, sir, — Napoleon Bonaparte, I repeat, — a man, although short in stature (whose average weight at any one time did not exceed 135 lbs. avoirdupois), who did this; and how, Mr. President? Simply, sir, simply by the use of intoxicating liquors. For, sir, when the Spanish chivalry of France was about to lie down and die on the bare and dilapidated shores of Russia, we read that N. Bonaparte telegraphed to the English monarch, Henry VIII., for a cargo of intoxicating liquors ; and giving these to his ill-clad men, he put new spirits into them, and they nobly achieved their independence from the Russian yoke of Turkish tyranny.

"Was it not for a worthy object that Alexander the Great crossed the roaring Rubicon and startled with his mighty voice the reindeers and fleet antelopes of Gaul? Then did he give utterance to that Latin proverb, 'Omnis Gallis divisa est in partes tres,' which means in our language, 'Wine makes glad the heart of man.'

"But the swiftly flying moments bid me cease my harangue, and I will now close as I began in the touching language of John Q. Milton, 'Sink or swim, survive or perish, I give my heart and hand to this vote.'"

The young man felt the importance of the hour. His preparation had been complete, and no trick of gesture or absurdity of vocal extravagance was omitted.

It was not to be imagined that John swallowed the speech without some inward qualms. Some of the students who were not admitted into the confidence of the conspirators in their excess of envy sought to raise the sceptical element in the young man's nature. John wavered, for example, on the description of Demosthenes as the "insatiate orator;" but he was assured, with the calmness that carries conviction, that the word "insatiate" was the name of a tribe of Indians in Africa, called the "Insatiates," distinguished among the tribes for their activity and prowess, so that the word, following the law of philological development, had come to stand as the synonym of "action," "force," "movement." Demosthenes was pre-eminently the orator of "action," and therefore the adjective "insatiate" was used with singular appropriateness.

A young marplot in the Virgil class had intimated that the Latin sentence "Omnis Gallis, etc.," was mistranslated, and John brought his doubts to his faithful friend Bragg. With ill-concealed surprise Bragg explained the impossibility of a mistake. John's informant was the dunce of his class, and his knowledge of Latin was proverbially meagre. "You know very well," said Bragg, "that Omnis means wine." John said of course he knew that word was right. "Then even an English scholar must know that the Latin verb gallio, gallere, galliri, etc., means 'to do,' 'to accomplish,' 'to make.'" John confessed that he had never doubted the second word; and so word by word the legend was translated, the words in Latin and English by a fortunate coincidence being the same in number, and the young man went away with his last doubt removed. The words "idiotically" and "ignoramously," which even John's credulous nature would have rebelled at, were not in the original notes, but were inserted just previous to the speech, when, under the stress and confusion of his excitement, these last touches were added, as crowning glories whose beauty would have been marred and probably eliminated by rehearsal.

The audience was convulsed, of course; but as John, bending the knee and with clasped hands as if in prayer, turned his fresh, fair face heavenward during the recitation of his Latin sentence, there was no sign in him of any emotion save that of triumph.

It was difficult longer to keep up the delusion. Relations of such intimacy had been established that it was not easy to shake him off. The boys had laughed themselves out; and so, with that irony of ingratitude which belongs to fallen human nature, a copy of the young man's speech, with marginal notes, was sent over the hills to the home of his parents, and the young orator was summarily recalled to the old farm.

Several years went by. The young conspirators, belying the promises of their youth, were fast merging into respectable citizens. The counting-house of one of the mills of Massachusetts contained one of them; legend said that some of the staid professions claimed others; while the young man Bragg, now a reputable practitioner, not far away, was rapidly coming into fame as a country doctor.

Riding along one day through the village which had been the home of the young orator, the doctor saw walking before him a stranger, and, after the hospitable manner of the country, drew up his horse and invited him to ride. As the stranger turned, the affrighted doctor saw that it was John. The rawness of youth had solidified into the massive strength of manhood, and the man of science had heard in many ways of the ominous threats of mutilation and murder that John had uttered against the conspirators. However, with placid face hiding an apprehensive spirit, the doctor dwelt with conspicuous volubility on the character of the country and the general run of the weather. But the thoughts of his companion wandered. He sat in dreamy meditation. A strange light, half of remembrance, was in his eye, and there was an appearance of abstraction, as if in the memory some half-forgotten thing was being sought for.

At last he exclaimed, "Is your name Bragg?"

Gulping down, with convulsive agony, his conscience and his fears, the doctor answered, "No! my name is Brown, James Brown."

His companion was silent, as if but half convinced. A pause ensued, in which the trembling doctor vainly tried to resume the topic of the weather; but John was busy with his thoughts.

At last he said, "Were you ever a student at Woodstock?"

"Woodstock," thoughtfully answered the physician. "Did I not come through such a town this morning? A large fine town with an open square?"

"Yes, but that is not the place. South Woodstock. I mean, — a little village five miles this side."

The doctor mused again, — "thought he remembered the place, and was struck with the appearance of an academy-looking building, which he supposed was a church. No, he had never been there to school; had always lived on a farm, and had had but few advantages of education, a thing which in his vocation as the keeper of a country store he found constantly operating to his disadvantage."

The inquiries of the baffled John ceased. He was not satisfied, but he was quieted. He merely remarked, in a subdued tone, but with a dark, malignant, revengeful look in his eyes, "I used to know a man by the name of Bragg when I was at that place at school, and I would like to meet him. He did n't treat me just right. I never saw two men who looked so much alike!"

Still with a faint tremor of apprehension the genial doctor remarked that "he had often been taken for other men, and it was singular how strong the resemblance often was between entire strangers."

By this time the village had been reached, and the passenger, with quiet thanks, but still with that mysterious, searching, baffled look upon his face, alighted.

The traveller's horse moved on, the pulse of the practitioner gradually recovered its normal beat, the color came back slowly to his cheeks, and like one who had escaped some overshadowing peril, the solitary man drove on his way.

The youthful orator is already past middle life. He has become a shrewd, keen, successful man of business, held in honor among his neighbors and warm repute among his friends. The school-days at the Green Mountain Institute are remembered by him with pleasure; and he tells, probably with pardonable emendations, the story of the night in the debating society, when in the days of his fresh youth he delivered the solitary speech which was destined to make him famous in the annals of the school as "Orator John."

MAYBROOK FARM.

WE had always sighed for a farm. Was there ever a man brought up on a farm who did not wish to end his days on one? No matter if he hated it as a boy, he always dreamed of it as a man. Of course, ministers' children are not brought up on special farms or anywhere else in particular; but then there was farm blood in our ancestry, and we have the instinct by inheritance. A friend, who once edited the "New England Homestead," in answer to the questions of his subscribers as to how he knew so much about farming, used to say, "Why, I lived twelve years on a farm." "I did not tell them," he slyly said to us, "that they were the first twelve years of my life."

Well, we spent a portion of our life on a farm. Not a great portion, but still enough to get a love for it. Of course we could not master the whole science of farm work in the two weeks, but we learned the rotary motion of the grindstone, that the cows are milked at night, and that the sun gets hot toward noon. We followed the hay-cart with a hand-rake, and in the wake of the mower cut down the burdock in the fence corners. The contract was entirely unselfish on our part, for it specified that we were to get just what we earned; and at the conclusion of the engagement, the farmer, who was a cobbler on wet days, gave us a pair of shoes. They have lain heavy on our conscience ever since as an overpayment; but the farmer's wife and daughters bullied him into it, and saw no reason that we should be made to suffer because we left off early, especially as we made it up by beginning late.

So our readers will see how natural it was that we should be ambitious for a farm. To be sure, the neighbors, whose back windows overlooked our yard, never perhaps suspected the dream we cherished. Cynical members of our own unappreciative household had been wont to remark that they should think that people who aspired to a farm would at least occasionally work out their bucolic tastes on the land they had; but it was not a paltry garden to which we aspired. We yearned for a farm of lordly acres; and so through the years we have been wont to dream that when we came to our "Castle in Spain," it would be upon a farm; and while we dreamed, the weeds beneath our study windows grew rankly and merrily.

Well, we have come to it at last, and Maybrook completely fills the outlines of our dream. It was not a common farm we sighed for, with stony fields and

broken fences, and yards much littered; with house unfurnished and barns disordered; with herds of common stock and horses sullen with ignoble blood. It was a farm that was rich in splendid outlooks, with meadows starred with flowers and pavilioned with lordly branches; with gleaming brooks and woods that had deep shadows in them; a farm rimmed with hills, with wide-eyed cattle feeding in the sun, and horses swift of instinct to find the beauty that hides in grass-grown roads. It was a farm wherein the processes of labor should be unobtrusive. The mower's scythes should cut for the rhythm of their music, and the grass should change to hay for the odor's sake; the cows should feed in the meadows not for the milking, but for the landscape; and the farmer should count his acres fruitful if the crop of beauty was abundant, and esteem his trees not for the lumber they would mill, but for the shadows they would cast.

Of course we know that butter does not grow in the buttercups, that crops must be planted and tended with much homely labor, and that if men will eat, the farmer must toil with calloused hand and sweat of face. But men need beauty as well as bread, and the farm we sighed for was one that grew both of these crops, and somewhere we knew that there was such a place; in Arcady, perhaps, but somewhere on the earth, or in the land of dreams. We did not think that we should find it at Maybrook, in the Harlem Valley.

But here it is. Not that this is any enchanted place, where trees are raised for their shadows, and the grass is grown for the daisies. The cows that are feeding in the meadows are distilling their cuds into merchandise at the rate of twenty quarts at a milking; and in the carts which are winding through the fields

as though they were there only to give the landscape life, there is good honest compost for the corn. We half suspect that the waste water from the fountains feeds the cattle-troughs beyond; and we know that behind the hedges, across the brook from the conservatory with its orchids and exotics, there is a kitchen-garden. Our friend who lives at Maybrook is not the kind of man to be content to feed on dreams and moonbeams; and has he not told us that "the farm pays"? — although the book-keeping which brings the balance on the credit side we suspect is of that peculiar kind that men invent when they have unquiet consciences and wives whom they desire to propitiate. But we have not told anything about Maybrook yet.

It is set in the midst of the Harlem Valley, seventy miles or so northward from New York. Beyond the sloping hills on the eastward side is the Housatonic, and beyond the western rampart is the Hudson. When the Lord parcelled out the beauty for the three valleys, the Harlem helped itself first, and the other valleys took what was left over. A mile or so above the village, the road which has skirted the great plain turns eastward, running in a bewitching curve beneath an avenue of maples, and so along a hundred rods or more, until it comes to the upward end of the great field which stretches unbroken southward to the village; and this is Maybrook. The house itself is rather a villa than a house, with broad piazzas and tower on the eastward side, and many rooms within, as befits the home of hospitality.

But it is the farm, and not the house, that we set out to tell about; and we shall not linger to tell of the art and luxury gathered here within this pleasant home. The house is set within the midst of lawns, as green and lustrous as the fields one sees in England on the Midland Road, with winding roads and graceful shrubberies, and flower-beds kept bright with blooming flowers. There are the greenest hedges round the great yard, not high, as though intrusion were warded off, but low and green, as if to say, "We want to share with every passer-by the beauty of our lawns and flowers." There are trees set in just the place that Nature would have chosen had she been asked her mind, and graceful fountains are where the wind can catch the spray and weave it into draperies of mist. Backward, stretching through the lawns, is a path which leads to the greenhouse set far up, and on each side there are great lines of blooming geraniums, looking for all the world like the scarlet-coated lines of soldiers through which the Queen of England walks when she enters one of the royal buildings. Midway in this yard of many acres there is a brook, which comes from the woods beyond, flows through Maybrook Farm, and empties into the Weebatuck, half a mile away. It is twenty feet or more in width, and bounded by the low walls which rise to the level of the lawn. It is a mountain stream; and not a gurgle nor a murmur that it learned in the woods will it yield or disguise, but it sings on over the rocks as fresh and beautiful as when it was born in the cavern of the woods beyond. In the midst of it there is a great elm, seemingly large enough for the building of a frigate. You shall run your line for more than a hundred feet before you can measure the diameter of its shadow on a summer's day. It keeps its roots in the brook, as though it loved it; and the brook keeps it fresh and green, willing to pay the toll, which the tree drinks up, for the sake of the shadows which keep it cool and remind it of the forest from which it came.

Crossing the road we enter the great farm. For a quarter of a mile, by a winding road as smooth as a city parkway, we come down to the great barns by the banks of the Weebatuck, where the hundred Holsteins live. When the millennium comes, and cows like other folks get all their rights, and the aristocrats among them wish to build a kind of club-house for the nabobs of their kind, they will send a committee to Maybrook for their plans. It is the summer-time, and this is the winter palace. The Holsteins have taken the field, and the barn is sweet with lime and lavender.

We came to Maybrook to help our friend gather in his summer crops. We are not visitors or idlers, but workers here. We should be ashamed to be drones when all the world around us is at work. Maybrook has double crops, — the grass that makes the milk and the grass that makes flowers; the trees that make lumber and the trees that make shadows;

the water that cools the milk and the water that sings in the brook and makes mist-wreaths around the fountains. We are simply to be counted among the farm-hands; but because there are double crops the work must be done in double gangs, and we are at work

on the invisible harvests. We gather the music and the melody, the odors and the sunshine: we have charge of the brook to see if its songs are all in tune; we watch the flowers to see if their dyes are fast and true, and watch the Holsteins, with no thought of their udders, but only to see if they keep their backs of ebony just where the sun will make them shine like beetles' wings. So, of course, we cannot tell the things which do not come within our province. We know that Maybrook comprises six hundred acres; that the Holsteins have a pedigree that goes back, for aught we know, to the Norman Conquest; that they run milk like the rivers of Canaan, and that like all other folks of great degree and ancient lineage, they come awfully high; that the milk is sent twice a day over the hills to the factory; that it goes in big cans and is drawn by a span of horses that carry their docked tails as airily as though they were hauling the American aristocracy instead of dragging milk; that some of the cows give twenty quarts at a time, and would give more if the milkers were not ashamed to be so mean as to take it; that the aggregate of milk sold is in the tons, we forget how many, either ten or a hundred, perhaps between the two. There are hospitals for the sick, private apartments for the convalescents, and great yards where they can take their sun-baths in winter. In fact, the Holsteins seem to have everything except a reading-room and a gymnasium; and these they would doubtless have, with a five-cent coffee-house thrown in, if there were any poor among them.

We are afraid that those of our indulgent readers who are themselves wrestling with the farm-hand problem will do us the injustice to think that as farm-hands we are not really earning the board which is our wages. But we can assure them that we are no idlers. The men in the other gang do not work longer hours. When the milkers go to their task we go to ours; we go out and see the dew go off, and note the roses that have opened; we let the birds sing to us, and take the messages that the brook has brought down in the night out of the heart of the woods. The other men, who run the mowers in the field, have easy task here at Maybrook compared with ours. Nature offers no resistance to the gathering of the crops they seek. But she hides from us, and makes us gather our harvests by stealth. The Holsteins need no wooing; but these sprites that have a message for us hide in the woods when they hear our footfall, and we must coax them forth, and entice them to tell their story.

One canno invade the silences of Nature with boisterous sound, nor seize her riches with a burglar's violence. It is necessary to despoil her by indirection. Margaret Fuller used to say that "Nature would not be stared at," and he who would find the secrets of Nature's life must look as the astronomers do, when with the naked eye they look at a star: they see it best by looking at the one that is nearest it. And so while with a chatter and noise the other farmhands at Maybrook do their work, we must keep silence, that we may interpret the silences of Nature, bringing to the fields and woods, the brook and the tree, that inner vision which alone interprets Nature, thus heeding well the old counsel of the seer, to

> "Seal up both the eyes
> And send them to the heart."

And then is it as easy as mowing and reaping to hear the " sweet voices that in the grasses talk," and strain the heart's inner hearing that it may catch the sounds with which " Nature is vocal to him that hath the listening ear."

Moreover, the other men have no territory for their work besides the six hundred acres of Maybrook's fields and woods. But we must climb

the clouds with the sunset to find the texture of the purple and golden draperies with which it robes the skies; we must drive over the hills where, in the nooks of pasture walls, Nature has made her richest tangles of weed and brier; we must skirt the gorge of the woods to see where Nature in fern and flower has hid her masterpieces. And the night brings no cessation of work for us; for if the day uttereth speech, the night showeth knowledge. There are odors that are distilled only under the pressure of the night air. The moonlight spiritualizes Nature and compels new interpretations. Altogether, it is a busy life that we are leading here at Maybrook. The crops that we have come to gather are ripening fast in these glorious summer days. The hills, the broad field, the lawns and flowers, the hedges and the running brook, the drooping elm-branches, the deep recesses of the woods, where the ferns and bushes rock the cradle of the brook, — all these, and the uncatalogued beauties of this fair Maybrook, invite us to loiter and listen, and let our souls delight themselves with fatness.

And then beyond it all, when the day has been crowded to the brim with beauty, and the eye is weary with the burden of its delights, and the heart needs quietude that it may put away forever upon its walls the pictures of the day, the night comes with the social joys of Maybrook. Within the home, adorned with all that art and literature, music and culture, can give, or within the little building which, made into a single room of beauty, spans the brook, we gather when the darkness comes, to talk of the day's delights and plan new joys for the coming day. How fairy-like it seems, this stately room, with frescoed ceilings and walls of oak, and every device which ingenious art could fashion, to create a room of beauteous comfort here, and set it over the brook between the lawns and in the shadow of the elm. And so delightful nights follow delicious days here at our Maybrook home, while the brook sings on, and the world goes round, and we sink to rest no longer to dream of our Castle in Spain, but to rejoice that we have come to it at last, and that its name is Maybrook.

THE HARVEST OF A QUIET EYE.

OF course, in coming to Maybrook to help our friend gather in his crops, we could not at once do a full stint of work. Even the other men, who are harvesting the hay, have been obliged first to harden palm and muscle. We have had no desire to loiter at our work, but in the kind of harvesting that we have come to do, we cannot either force the crops or drive the workmen. If we would have the new birds come in our hearts and build their nests, we must open our windows and let the old birds fly out.

So thus far we have been preparing for our work. We have caught snatches of the songs the brook sings, have listened for a moment to the murmuring of the leaves, and glanced at the shadows that are marching up and down the hills; we have tried our muscles, as it were, as the mowers test their scythes before the day's work. But "the world is too much with us" yet. The roar of the year's life not yet has died to silence; the old birds not yet have made way for the nesting of the new tenants.

In coming back to Nature, one has something of the feeling that he experiences in going back to his childhood's home. The old associations seek to enter the heart, but they find other occupants, and they refuse to speak and we refuse to hear in the presence of strangers. There is always in our first meeting with Nature a sense of disappointment. The haunting voices of the world distrust the silence which is Nature's speech; and as lovers, meeting after separation, miss the expected rapture until they braid anew the subtile threads of fellowship which the alien world has broken, so Nature at first is silent and unresponsive, and we must let the world's echoes die away before we find complete restoration in the old love.

But now it is time for our full work of harvesting; and while the other workmen are at their tasks we shall go through the fields, following the brook, and shall gather

"The harvest of a quiet eye."

Had the day been other than it is, we should not have come here for our work. Had it been bright with blue skies, and brilliant with flashing sunbeams, we should have climbed the hills and harvested the rolling clouds and the exhilarations of waving grasses. Had it been a day of mists, we should have gathered the perfumes that the pressure of the mists distils; but this is Forest Day, and as surely as the fish say, on days that are overcast, "We will graciously be caught to-day," so the woods have now their heaviest crops, and woe betide us if we reap in the meadows when Nature has her harvests ready for us in the woods. We think that we must have read somewhere that Nature creates days for special insights and outlooks. Does not Emerson tell us that the scholar must await the right hour for reading Plato's "Timœus;" that God makes special days when the elect of the ages graciously draw near to men and are responsive to man's questionings, but when their hour of elevation is gone they become but dumb oracles again!

This is Forest Day. The slumberous air was made for the insects of the woods. How they will sing and frolic and spread their wings! Were it Mountain Day, their music would be lost in the whispering winds; were it Ocean Day, the air were too heavy for spreading out the glories of all their gossamer vanities. The leaves will be alive, and yet they will have time for pleasant gossipings. The ferns will carry each graceful curve in clear relief, while every frond and plume will have a background of gently waving grasses and flossy tapestries of vine and tendril.

Do our readers care to know something of the place where we are to gather our harvests? If they will but go into the nearest wood they shall see what place it is in which we are set to harvest; for the woods of Maybrook, though they are richly dowered, are not unlike other woods that hide a world of wonders from us within sight of half our homes, while we comprehend them not.

There is a brook which comes down out of the mysteries of the hills. It flows over stones which have been ebonized by suns, and scarred by floods; it murmurs among silvered pebbles and rocks from which float tresses as long as those the Spartan maidens combed on the morning of the day their lovers held the pass. What a wondrous thing is a brook! Mysterious in its birth, elusive in its death; cradled in the mists of the hills, lost in the mists of the sea; but between the two vague boundaries of its being it hews its channel, waters the meadows, swings the hammer of the forge, turns the factory shaft, floats the wheels of commerce, and bears away the city's waste.

By-and-by this brook will serve the other hands, who, with us, are set to gather the crops of Maybrook. The gardener will divert its channel for his plants, the hostler for his hose, the foreman for his troughs. Have we not equal rights with these? So we shall put phantom wheels within the brook, build our mills among the branches, and do our weavings here; and we shall let the brook turn the lathes and be the lapidary to polish these pebbles. While we are at our harvestings and the brook is helping us, we shall not compel it to make merry for us, as the Philistines did their slave, but shall simply hear its music,

knowing that, gossip as it is, it will tell the inmost secret of its heart, if we but listen. There is, of course, a road that follows the brook upward to the old homestead of its birth. Green-carpeted it is, with mossy rocks between its ruts, and there are great ledges on these hills which bound the gorge, trying to look sternly at us; but kindly Nature, in smoothing out the wrinkles of her frown, has left veils of verdure, behind which, if the ledges frown, they must do so unseen. Then there are great trees, which have written the record of half a century on bark and trunk, somehow knowing that this day would come, and we should come to read their story.

But we shall not tell too minutely the things we gather here. You will never know, most curious friend, the names of the rocks, the dip of the strata here, nor shall we tell you the names of the trees, or the titles that the flowers have. Must we enumerate each separate wheat-head that we gather in our harvestings? Cannot we enjoy the trees without an estimate of the cubic feet they will measure at the mill? Are the strata of the ledges more than their moss and lichen? Are we like a mere botanist, who misses the blossom that he may count the seeds in the pod, who spoils the flower to find its name, and esteems its name more than its beauty?

It is heresy, we know, to say it, but we believe that this dissecting of Nature makes one incapable either of understanding or of loving her. You can no more carry your botanizing box with you to the woods, and learn the flowers, than you can study the birds with a rifle. Does not the great seer of Nature ask,—

"Hast thou named all the birds without a gun?
If not, thou knowest not the birds."

The Greeks were poor anatomists, but it was their chisel that carved Venus and Apollo. The tyro in our modern schools could teach them the laws of crystallization, the processes of vegetable growth; but they saw dryads in the woods, found angels in stone, and made the marble breathe. We have no contest with these wooden-hearted pedants, who can give the catalogue of all the ologies; who have microscopes, but not eyes; who know the names of all the flowers, but never have learned the mystery of a single blossom; who have analyzed the salts and acids in the earth, but never have felt the beat of its mighty heart or interpreted the movement of its splendid life. Only dead things can be dissected. You can never dissect your Apollo and find the glory of his being. Divide Venus into muscles and membranes, and you have lost her. We must come to Nature, when we woo her, not with the student's critical analysis, but with the ardor of the lover, if we would learn her secrets and feel the pressure of her throbbing life. Not that the student's analysis is, in itself, unwise; but it is incomplete. This surely is Yorick's skull, but unless you put back the quips and cranks, you have not Yorick here. Cæsar turned to clay was Cæsar still, but there was something that defied analysis, and that something ruled the world. Nature, like God, refuses to be analyzed. Not by searching shall she be revealed. Your microscopes are blinds, not windows; and in attempting to find Nature by dissections you miss her, like those of whom Lowell speaks, who "cannot see their forests for their trees."

We cannot tell the things that we have harvested on this summer day in these woods of Maybrook. Why, the whole beauty of the world is here! Our friends who wished to see the wonders of the earth pitied us, no doubt, when they crossed the sea. But we are pitying them to-day. Why were they not wise enough to know that we need not go up and down the earth to find its beauty? Shakespeare sat down in the field beside his native stream, and the world brought its beauty to him. Wherever there is an eye to see, there the fairies come and dance.

The crowds are at Paris, but we have cooler shades and larger visions here, in these woods at Maybrook. There are clever weavings there, but there are finer weavings here in the gossamer that makes the spider's bridge between the leaves. There are carvings in the Parisian bazaars; but will the châlets of Switzerland show anything to equal the curling crests of the tiny wavelets in this mountain brook? How crude is the lace-like silver work of Milan compared with these birchen trees "clothed in white samite"! These cloud draperies, these pendent vines, are richer than the sheen of Lyons' silk and the Gobelin tapestries. The stars on which we shall look to-night will outnumber the lamps of the Rue de Rivoli; and the palaces of Versailles will not reveal such frescos as these that are over us in the twining branches of these forest shades of Maybrook. Indeed, we pity, to-day, our friends who, with gaping wonder, are staring at the Luxor column. How modern it is! Why, those figures on it are only of the yesterdays of two thousand years ago! Come here to Maybrook and see something old! These rocks and ledges are as old as the earth, and these messages of the wrinkled rocks were ages old when Egypt lay untenanted beside the Nile. For our Notre Dame we have these larger aisles of God's first temples; for our Eiffel Tower we have the hills, "rock-ribbed and ancient as the sun;" for our Louvre we have the larger masterpieces of sun and cloud, the forest and the brook; and the meanest weed or flower we have at Maybrook shames the rarest handiwork of all the exhibitors at Paris. Do not pity us, poor globe-trotters. We are pitying you.

We wonder if, when those who have hunted round the world in search of beauty come home again, they will still be able to enjoy the beauty that is in humble things; if those who have seen Vesuvius still can love to see the smoke rise up from the chimney of a humble home! Beauty is not at all a thing of measurements, and no genuine love of beauty will

permit wonder at the great to destroy love for the sweet simplicity of common things. The Alps have been enemies, not friends, if they have wooed our heart from Monadnock and Kearsarge. Monadnock is unkind if it changes the pasture slope of the hill that is part of the old farm into something common and neglected. Beauty is not a thing of rivalries. Its language is broken into no dialects; it is a universal speech. He who loves Nature, loves her in all her vestures; her royal draperies only make us welcome the homespun garments of common life, as the glories of the Alps educate the Swiss cottagers to fill their windows with delicate flowers. The true lover of Nature not only can feel the great throb of the river flowing to the sea, the stir of its cities, the might of its commerce, but also the splendor of the fields and flowers through which it flows, the beauty of the primrose by the river's brim. Wordsworth was one of the truest lovers that Nature ever had. But her ordinary life was not made unattractive by her larger splendors, and though he said: —

> "The sounding cataract
> Haunted me like a passion; the tall rock,
> The mountain, and the deep and gloomy wood,
> Their colors and their forms, were then to me
> An appetite."

Yet so does love, like the sea, fill places infinitely large and small, that he also confessed that —

> "To me the meanest flower that blows, can give
> Thoughts that do often lie too deep for tears."

There is in this unity of beauty a revelation of higher things. The wonders of Nature reveal the power and majesty of Him who rideth upon the wings of the wind; but the lesser beauties, which lie in the gateways of our own homes, which are all around us in these Maybrook woods, speak of the Love which is acquainted with us in all our ways. For us, at least, as we sit here in these woods, and gather " the harvest of a quiet eye," we have ready our choice, if we must make election, between the greater or the lesser beauty of the world. Let Alps and Apennines be blotted out, we shall keep our little mounts of vision, the pasture slope fragrant with the breath of childhood. Silence Niagara's roar, but leave for us the music of the brook within our familiar woods. We can live without the marshallings of armies, the pomps and pavilioned splendors of life; but life cannot be lived without its homely joys, the sweet domesticities of friendship. We can spare the king's proclamations better than the lover's whisperings. When Nature speaks to us it is not with mouthings of great words, but in the heart's simplest language; and when God wishes to reveal the inmost secrets of his providence, he cries not from the mountains, but walks with man in the silences of the cool of the day, speaking not with the thunder but with the voice that has stillness.

And yet, as the grass in the meadows of Maybrook,

where the other harvesters are working, is tough to the dull scythe, so in these higher harvestings of beauty, the crops are gathered best by him who brings to the gathering the best implements and the largest zeal. The field of beauty is a thing of visions: and to read the soul of Nature, we must bring the inner vision of a soul attuned to her. The old proverb tells us to " put love within the heart and it shall add a precious seeing to the eye;" and, after all, it is not only love that makes the world go round, it is love that can best interpret the causes and the issues of its revolutions.

So the hours have speeded, while we have been gathering the crops that grow in Maybrook's woods. The other workers in the lower fields can bring their harvestings in loaded wagons to the barns, but we go back from our toilings without a wheel to carry our spoils. Yet who shall say that for the needs of life, its sustenance and growth, the woods of Maybrook do not grow as rich a harvest as its meadows?

THE HOUSE THAT PETE BUILT.

WE suppose that his real name is Peter, but he is always called Pete. It is hardly possible that any of our readers ever saw him, for he has seldom been away from home, and is only visible in summer, as he freezes up in winter like other hibernating creatures.

Of course we mean "Pete the carpenter." Like many other discoveries that have been of service to the world, his origin is mythical: he claims to be of French extraction, and it is probable that he drifted over from the Canadian shore in the glacial period; at any rate, he is here, as much a part of the scenery of Summerland as the rocks and trees. Men may come and men may go, but Pete stays on forever. In the old country he would be called a factotum; in dramatic parlance, a general utility man; in Masonic phrase, a permanent jewel; but to us he is simply "Pete the carpenter."

None of us knows his antecedents and none knows his destiny, except that he will last as long as there is a board to saw or a nail to drive in Summerland.

When falls the world, then falls the island; and when the island falls, then falls Pete. His age is as uncertain as that of a maid gone thirty. There is no way of arriving at it, as we cannot cut him open like a tree to count the rings, nor make him open his mouth like a horse that we may inspect his teeth. He is one of those peculiar fellows whose age does not register itself. We have many such, who might be thirty or three hundred. Pete is such a one. In personal appearance he is hardly an Apollo, but then for that matter there are few of us who are. He is short in stature, with eyes set together like those of a squirrel. His legs are short, and were they put together upon the printed page, would be taken for a parenthesis. He has the gift of silence, but keeps ready answer for every question; and altogether he has a merry heart, and is as nimble in his wit as with his hands.

We do not know how it ever happened that he became a carpenter. In our confidential talks he has never told us where or when he learned his trade; we do not think he ever learned it, but nevertheless he has some of the elements of genius with a saw and plane. He can fit boards to any angle, and drive a nail at any inclination, can use his eye for a tape-line, and make a joint without a mortise-board. He can shake two boards together and make a closet in the twinkling of an eye, go over the rafters of a building like a cat, and can never be put to shame by any mechanical task, however impossible it may seem to other men. It is said of him, moreover, that he consumes his own shavings like one of the modern smoke-devouring engines, though we do not stake our reputation on the truth of this assertion. We know at least that he has other diet than his chips, for he uncovers his pail at high noon by the standard time, and rarely runs beyond the vespers for his tea.

He is also semi-amphibious, and can make a crib or repair a dock as well under water as on its surface, while with a boat he is master and can sail straight to his home with the wind in any quarter. The other day he carried us to the village, three miles away. The waves were foam-crested and the wind was high and boisterous; but our trust in him was unfaltering, and when he invited us into the cockle-shell which serves him for a boat, we went without a single fear. The sail was fitted to its place, and we went with the wind. There was no rudder, and he disdained the use of an oar, but by some mysterious skill steered his boat by the sail-rope he held: now it was loose, now taut; now he was on the seat, again upon the gunwale, again crouched on the bottom of the boat, but simply by his handling of the sail and his position in the boat, he shaped his course at will. Discovering at length that he was not steering by either oar or rudder, we asked him if he meant to tell us that he could carry us just where we wished to go without touching oar to water. Whereupon he simply asked us where we wished to land. We told him where we would have it, and the wizard Pete sent his boat like an arrow from a Tartar's bow to the very spot, not even touching oar at the last to make the landing at the dock.

This was the man that built our summer home. We do not know just why we built when we did, except that Pete was on the island and the other job he had was finished, and some law or fate ordained that it was our turn next. We had thought to break the thread of fate and demonstrate that some other could wield the saw and hammer on the island, and it was perhaps for such a purpose rather than ambition for a larger house that we essayed to build. We know at least that we engaged another builder; but the fates cannot be outwitted, and when the time for building came, there was Pete upon the rafters, so nimble-footed that we could not catch him and drive him off. We are not of that mulish kind of creature that cannot accept defeat; and never asking whether he had bribed or killed the other workman, we surrendered to the conqueror, only asking that he mercifully treat us. We did not design to build a palace or even a house of imposing size. We are not ambitious, and there are limits to our fortune. Something small and cheap, which could be finished in half the vacation season, so that we might have the using of it: this is what we asked of Pete. There are builders we have seen, who, before they build, closet themselves with architects and have, in finest traceries of india ink and other pigments, a plan of the building they will have. But Pete is the architect of his own buildings, — if not of his own fortune, — and is apt to be governed in his work by the length of the timbers and the condition of prospective jobs. So we paced off on the rocks where we would set the posts, and we made the framing according to some invisible plan of Pete's.

There are many advantages in building a house upon an inhabited island. The lumber has to be transferred in scows, which afford fine opportunities for muscular development. Then there are neighbors who take a hand, not perhaps in carrying of boards, but in planning. Each one has his own peculiar views as to where the windows, doors, and partitions ought to be; and where a builder is complaisant, and tries to please his friends, he is apt to have the pleasure of building half-a-dozen houses in getting one. We do not even wish to intimate that Pete the builder actually invited criticism that he might tear down to-day the work of yesterday. We only know that he was considered island property, and took his orders kindly from every source.

Our doors and windows were of the migratory kind, here to-day, somewhere else to-morrow. We tried to please our friends, and so we shifted as the women wished. Of course we did not get along, but then we had lots of fun, and our friends and neighbors learned the elements of building at our expense. The fiction holds among our friends that we were the builder of our own house, but it is the veriest romance. We were only the puppet who sat upon the throne and paid the bills, while Pete was the autocrat behind the throne.

So the vacation drifted on. At first the work seemed to go with speed, for there were other houses yet to build. But when the building of these was put off, then progress ceased. This workman failed to come, that one was sick, though we half suspect that Pete drowned them in the going or the coming. We begged our neighbors to build their houses as they had planned, telling them that Pete was like these chronic old lovers who are never off with the old love till they are on with the new, that they were richer than we and ought to help us out; but they deserted us, and so the season drifted on, and Pete, like the blessed poor, threatened to be always with us.

Every day we worked at the side of Pete. We laid the floors and made all sorts of impossible squares and diamonds in the lattice-work, which were readjusted afterward by Pete. We laid battens on cracks, and put shingles on roofs, while we watched the sawing of every board for shelves and closets and did no little work of the cabinet sort on the interior finishing. To be sure, we had often to call Pete when we were perplexed as to how to turn a joint for a corner bracket, and it is possible that we did not greatly expedite the work; but then we showed our good intentions, and we worked for nothing.

We did not at the outset intend to praise ourselves, for our cottage home is the handiwork of Pete, but the painting is our own.

We had with us a friend, who lives with us in our island home, and is as the apple of our eye. Together we essayed to prime the building. We mixed our paint as best we could, with lead and oil, umbers, vermilions, yellows, and other colors, making a hue that pleased us well, though it was a color never seen on land or sea.

So we painted; but when the pot was empty, and we tried to duplicate the color, we had forgotten the combination, and though we tried with tears we could not bring it. Then the colors began one by one to be exhausted; and when our work was finished, we had a house like Joseph's coat, ranging from richest olive to chocolate, mauve, lavender, old gold, peach-color, and a dark shade of white. We think the work must have been well done, for we understand that it attracted a good deal of attention. One of our neighbors said that in the fall, after we had left, they brought parties on excursion trains to see it. We

THE HOUSE THAT PETE BUILT. 57

regret to say that we were the victim of that unfortunate trait in human nature which is never content

to see success without envy. Our island home has many roofs of house and veranda, and we frescoed these with red. We did not claim that we were either the glass of fashion or the mould of form as we lay sprawled upon the roof. We were not arrayed perhaps as Solomon in all his glory; but at least we did a job that has stood the test of snows and rains, and is not even now streaked over-much. Yet it has been asserted that instead of using brushes, we used to climb to the ridge-pole of the roof, upset the paint, and slide down in the torrent; and for proof of it, our maligners claim that the streaks on the roof correspond in width to our own person. When we resent the accusation, they dare us to the measurement. We point to the brush we used, but they retort by pointing to the overalls we wore; and we are pained to state that friends to whom we have related our grievance tell us that the overalls if not the facts are certainly against us.

We did have one serious misadventure. The house has not a mortgage, but it has an ell. We were at work upon its roof. The ladder was long; the roof was low. Of course the proper way to do was to go up the staging of the house, then climb to the staging on the roof and do our work. Now, if we could go a little above the lower staging we could step to the upper one, which thing we tried. But the law of gravitation was against us. The ladder tipped, and we came down. The fall was not great, but the fall of a man with a pot of red paint in his hand does not have to be great to be disastrous. The bulk of the paint went down our right arm; it quietly turned the angles of elbow and shoulder and then gently percolated over our entire person. We could have easily doubled our income if we had consented to supersede the tattooed man in the greatest show on earth, for we were colored with a higher degree of art. There is nothing in the realm of Nature so absolutely cold as red metallic roofing paint. We know it. We would not have minded this little episode; we lost the paint, or rather we did not exactly lose it,—we had it, though not in just the place we had designed. We had on a red shirt in place of a white one, and we were not the first individual who had painted his person. But then there were below us half a score of loafers, ministers, island owners, and others, who had been making a practice of coming over and jeering at us. When they saw we were not killed they laughed as never mortals laughed before. They have described the incident with other embellishments than that afforded by the paint, and they hesitate to forget it as they ought. Fearing lest they may go to selling county rights, we give the plain, unvarnished tale, that our traducing may not enrich those who scoffed at us.

Well, the season passed on, and the house was finished, Pete remaining with us to the last and bringing away his tools on the same steamer that took our clothes. Two years passed on, the unfinished cottage with its polychromatic decorations being the wonder if not the admiration of all beholders. At length on a certain night we reached the island coming from the east, and promptly next morning, at seven o'clock, Pete appeared, coming from the west.

In our plannings for the finish we had set down a week of Pete, but a month is passed, and his kit of tools is still unmoved. Once at least on Saturday we discharged him, but on Monday morning he appeared with his new-washed apron ready for another week. He is at this writing working for the island; but when the dock is finished, we expect he will return to us, as cats return to their old homes, — in fact, so long as Pete survives, we do not expect that we shall live in a finished house. But then he is an honest fellow, who gives good measure for his pay, and does his work in hearty, wholesome fashion, and never yet have we had reason to wish that we could see the last of him. He bears with all our failings, and rarely groans when we strike a nail with his freshly sharpened saws; and a man who can bear such things has in him the possibility of sainthood.

The house that Pete built, or that he is building, is a little thing, but it is very dear to us, for it nestles beneath the great pine-tree, and is less than twenty feet away from the river's ripples. From its piazzas, islands are visible and great reaches of this stateliest of rivers; and already we have lived long enough within it to love its rooms, and to dream of it when the weary work of the great world presses sore upon us. Friendship has woven some of its garlands over it, and it has become dear to us with the sanctity that makes a house a home. As the years go on we shall hope to come to its grateful shelter; but we do not expect, as we do not desire, ever to come when we shall not find awaiting us its architect and builder, Pete, ready not indeed to finish, but to continue the work of building. And not until some returning glacial drift shall carry him away, shall we ever expect that we can say our house is finished.

OLD YEAR'S REVERIES.

IT is the last night of the old year. The sound of hurrying feet within the street has ceased, for the night is waning toward the hour which shall usher in the new day and the new year. The Sabbath preparation has been completed, and for a long time we have sat by our study-fire musing over the changes of the year. Its gayeties and friendships, its toils and victories, its seasons of effort and of rest, have all passed by, as though out of the fire that burns before us some magic hand had brought the relics of the past. We are not old in years, and not yet do we find our pleasures to be of the past; the glad to-day is better than our yesterday, and the to-morrows that are coming will bring larger blessings than the past has wrought. And yet the old year's fading hours, by some necromancy of their own, change in their retrospection the dream of youth into the memories of age. So to-night we have been living in the past, and if we have thought of the days that are to be, it has been with wonder as to what change and marvel they will bring. Not changes in the outward world, the swift surprises of its business or its life of trade and thought, but changes in the friendships of our lives, and the pleasant fellowships of being. We know not why it is that this last night of the year should bring around us thus the brooding memories of all the years of life. It is not because we have taken down from its familiar place the old and put up the new calendar; nor is it because with idle sentiment we have been wont to esteem times and seasons. Every night closes an old year, and every day marks an epoch in many lives. But memory to-night has been unlocking all its stores, and revealing in the firelight the secrets of forgotten days. Old friends long gone have burnished recollection, and the fellowships of far-off days have stirred remembrance like music heard in dreams.

For us, as yet, life ought to be a thing of anticipations, for youth not yet is wholly past; but when memory is our only guest, age is not a thing of years, and now to-night, when thought is wholly of the past, we can enter into sympathy with the old who live in the long ago. There has always been to us a deep significance in the splendid imagery of Moore, which pictures him communing with the old memories, as one who treads alone the deserted banquet-hall, the lights gone out, the garlands dead, nothing left but the relics of the past. So it seems to the old who live in the memory of departed days; the earth is filled with farewells to the dying and mournings for the dead; and to-night the invisible guests who keep silent fellowship with us, while the sands of the old year's life run out, stir the memories which we thought were long since dead beneath the ashes of the long, long years.

We are creatures of our circumstances, and even our dreams are woven of our waking thoughts. It has been the "touch of a vanished hand" that has led us into retrospection; and when once the door of garnered memories is opened, all the past marshals its remembered friends. We have been much among graves of late, and it was but yesterday that we laid away all that was mortal of one who was closely allied to us in the bonds of friendship. We had known her for half her life, and not often is a life so radiant with loveliness.

She was dowried with a beauty of which none was unconscious but herself, and the outward tabernacle fashioned in such grace was illumined ever by a bounding elasticity and mobility of life that fascinated by its radiance. Wherever she touched a life, she gave the blessing that abundant joyousness of living brings, and acquaintance gave her admiration, and friendship love.

Wherever she was, she was the magnet that drew all hearts, and even envy could not withhold the homage that her genuineness compelled. She used often to come and sit within this very room where we write to-night, bringing some message or office of friendship; and when she had gone it seemed as if the windows had been opened and the breath of summer had entered, and the room was filled with the music of singing birds. Wherever one met her, — in the home, in the social gathering, in the street, — it was meeting the sunshine, for her life was light and warmth and love. She was full of high enthusiasms, and gave her heart without reserve to those she loved. There was something of idolatry in her affection for parents and the inmates of the old home; and to praise her husband or children was to make her face kindle with very ecstasy of pride. She carried into womanhood the artlessness of the girl; and the merry laughter of her childhood, which was like the breath of heaven to the weary-hearted, was the music with which she charmed her babes. Her friends could not easily learn to call her by other than her maiden name. When marriage came, the new name was added, yet we called her by the old one too. But all the seasons pass; and this bright life, which like a summer's day was crowned with the brightness of the sun, the music of the birds, the colors of the flowers, passed on. And so we buried her, and the flowers among which she rested before the altar where she had stood as a bride were not more beautiful than was the outward form whose loveliness death had not marred.

There are some who say that when the spirits are set free they go not far away from the friends they loved upon the earth. "Behold, we know not anything!" But in these fading hours of the old year's life it seems as if there sat before us here this one who is numbered among the saints in glory. We have no vision that we can see her, but as sleepers waken from unconsciousness when friends stand over them, we somehow feel that we are not alone as we watch the old year out beside our study-fire. There are others here with us, — friends on whose graves the flowers have turned brown, but who went away so little time ago that the blessed anointings which time gives, have not yet changed the poignancy of a new grief into " pleasant recollections." There are none who are yet apparelled in the flesh who are with us in our musings here. These are all of those who have gone on into the life where the years have no end; and whether it is memory that brings them near or the longing for the renewal of companionship, we feel that the very place is hallowed as though it were filled with the forms of angels. Within us there stirs a dim and tremulous thought, that if the spirit could only see eye to eye we might behold our room actually tenanted this night with those with whom once we walked in friendship on the earth. So are we conscious of companionship while yet we sit alone, that did we make passage from the old to the new year, as we cross rivers from shore to shore, we would gladly say, —

> "Take, O boatman, thrice thy fee,
> Take, I give it willingly;
> For, invisible to thee,
> Spirits twain have crossed with me."

What are not these last hours of the old year witnessing? The merchant is busy beneath the gaslight with his ledgers, balancing the gains and losses of the year. Watchers beside the sick, with apprehension born of fear, and a questioning that dares not frame itself into words, wonder if when the new year shall become old the imperilled loved one will yet be with them in the flesh. Mothers are whispering their prayers beside the cradle of their babes, and love is weaving its protections about those who sleep, unconscious of the thoughts that guard them. And not a few are in communion with those who have passed on since the year was young. The midnight air is vocal with their speech, and vision is bright with their remembered forms. They sing the old songs, their laughter cheers, the brightness of their presence is around us, and the place where we sit in meditation is made holy ground, as on a winter's day our room is freshened by the exhilarating air brought in the garments of our visitors. How many friends esteemed have sat here with us during the changes of the year, but never such a royal company as this that watches with us the old year out. For memory has a clever alchemy that blinds vision to unpleasant things; and not the least of the blessed ministries of death is the power it has to turn around the frailties of friends, and show the virtues hidden on the other side. And so the year has kept for us its sweetest lesson for the last. Memory does not cherish the dreams but the realities of life; and if the friends that we have loved had ceased to be, our hearts would not be cheated into cheerfulness by their remembrance. The flowers that live twine themselves into no wreaths for the blossoms that have fallen, the beasts build no monuments and have no commemorations for their dead, and the very care with which we cherish the poor dust that apparelled the spirits we love, bears witness to our instinct for immortality. We touch the inner life through the outward form, and memory cherishes the place of burial, form and feature, speech and deed, because it feels that life is still alive, and beyond death there is the living soul.

To-morrow you may come with your scepticisms of life beyond, and we will answer your doubts with our little logics; but to-night where is there room for scoffing doubt to sit with us, when out of the mysterious silence the immortals have come back to hang memory with garlands and fill our room with their radiant presence? It is a cruel hand that will destroy even a child's bright dream, and all of us are sad when the fairies cease to dance in the visions of our children. It cannot be that God, who satisfiest the desire of every living thing, would keep alive forever this yearning for continued life, place in the human heart the hunger for immortality, invest the soul with the elemental instinct for life, and doom us to nothing else than dust to dust! But mere continuance of being is not the measure of our dreams. It is that we shall have identity of life, consciousness, memory of the past, its friendships and its loves; that the broken threads of fellowship shall be woven again together, and we shall let our life drift on beside the currents that mingle with it here. The power that makes us conscious of ourselves makes us conscious of those about us; and unless eternity means recognition and reunion, it means unconsciousness, and this is only another word for annihilation.

It was only two nights ago that we looked down on the tranquil face of the friend that all our hearts esteemed. The lifelong smile was gone, and the beauty that had won so many hearts missed the illumination that had made it a thing of fascination. And yet we whispered to ourselves, "There is the certitude of our immortality." For where in all the universe is there such waste as this would be, if such loveliness and grace of life, the sunshine and the music, the brightness and glory of life, these precious things which are infinitely more costly than Nature's richest distillations, have come to their final end?

So passes out with us the old year, not in laments but in rejoicings, not in sorrow for the dead but in joy for the living, not in sadness at separations but in gratitude for unchanging friendships. We wear our outward life as a mask that hides us from each other; and until the corn of wheat falls into the ground and dies, it abideth alone. Death removes the barriers between the living, and when spirits are unclothed they see eye to eye. The life that is, at this dying hour of the old year, for not a few of us is not perhaps what it was when the year was new; but the life that is to be has larger allurements and is a sweeter thing than once it seemed.

In the old patrician houses there was one door which was never opened except when the dead were carried forth to burial. This old year's night for us has opened the door, and back again have come with joy the friends who went in tears, and with the music of their speech and the brightness of their presence they have revealed to us the secret that death is only a process in the way of life.

So let the old years go and the new years come! What matters it, since life goes on and on! Love is sovereign alike in all the world; and if we may sorrow at the old fashion of death, we may rejoice at the older fashion of our immortality. Thus we may take up the new year's march, as those who know that the way they tread leads them at last to the city that hath foundations whose maker and builder is God.

AN EVENING WITH THE NEGROES.

ON Liberty Street, in New Orleans, there is a church called Wesleyan Chapel, where the primitive negroes hold the old doctrines after the manner of their fathers. The street has narrow sidewalks, and is poorly lighted. A bell, not larger than that of a locomotive, from the stubby belfry was calling the sable saints to worship; and a large audience was present. We were inclined to be modest in our desires and to sit near the door, so that if occasion called we could easily retire; but the sexton insisted that we should come up among the "quality," and did not bring us to anchorage until we were seated on the anxious seats, with nothing between us and the platform but the chancel rail. The building was of fair size, with box-like galleries and square pews; a stove was in the middle of the building; and in the rear, around a parlor organ, was a choir of voluminous dimensions. The congregation was a free-and-easy one. The older dames and gossips were going from seat to seat in little visitings; the young people were chatting; and it seemed as though we had intruded on a colored picnic, so was the buzzing of a hundred visitors apparent all around us. People came in with baskets, little satchels, umbrellas, and packages, which they put around the platform in the freest manner possible. Mothers brought their children and placed them on the kneeling step before the chancel rail, until the whole was lined with these black blossoms. It was a most uncomfortable seat; and as the service progressed, one by one they nodded, toppled, and fell over on the step, seeing which the mothers would step out, put a faded shawl beneath their heads, and leave them to their slumbers.

Soon there was a sudden hush, and a large-sized man bustled in, and went upon the platform. Turning to his audience, he said, " Sing, sing ! don't talk when you come into church, but sing. I like to have you sing." The talking ceased; and an old half-blind negro, sitting in the side seats, with his coat tied together with a white string, started a plaintive hymn. The audience caught it up, and with wonderful melody the music was rendered. Silence followed, but only for a moment, for a woman's voice with weird effect began another hymn; for a moment she sang alone, then another voice joined, and still another, until, with an effect that was indescribable, the whole audience was singing a wild, melancholy air, — an old slave song, that might have been wrung out of the heart of bondage. There was no lack of music ; song succeeded song, all of them strange to our Northern ears, but of such tender melody as more than once bid the tears come to our eyes.

The hour had come for service; and the pastor rose and read a hymn, deaconing it off in the olden style. It was sung well, but it was evident that the favorite music was not written in the hymn-book. The sermon was on the text, "Now are we the sons of God," with emphasis on the word "now." We were originally children of wrath, but by adoption we have become children of God. The discourse was not without ability. It was ingenious in design and admirably adapted to the audience. He described the apostle as sitting by the shore of the "Ugene Sea," had much to say of "Abby Father," was inclined to make predatory excursions against the Baptists, and evidently was not tinctured with the New Theology heresy. It was really refreshing to hear the old-time doctrines in their unameliorated depravity; to hear the descriptions of a hell that had some burn to it. But the most lurid descriptions of hell fell on unheeding ears, while the glories of heaven created a perfect fusillade of hallelujahs!

A few of the quaint remarks of the preacher linger in the memory: —

"Some men say that some are elected to be saved, and some are elected to go to hell. I don't preach no such stuff as that. . . . A faith like that ain't worth a puck-horn; it is like the old man's rabbit, — some one cut off a piece, and the old man thought that it had shrunk. We don't want no such shrinking faith as that! . . . Religion without principle ain't worth a hill of beans. . . . You have got to be busy in heaven. Even the arkies and the high arkies all say, glory, glory, glory! . . . There are different kinds of Christians. There is the Sunday Christian, with a soul the size of a chick-a-dee; another who does n't pray. If he does pray, he is as lazy about it as the man who put in his provisions for the year, his ham and bacon, and then went in and said grace on the whole year's stock. Another has a soul so small that if you poured grace into it, it would n't rattle. Some men are so small that, when they shout hallelujah, their voice is such a little squeaky thing it would n't be heard round the corner on Glorification Street. I like these great souls, so big that when they get to heaven the rustling of their wings shakes the streets of the golden city."

The sermon was one of great power, with touches of rude eloquence, warmed with humor and quaint wit, which kept the people alert and earnest. The audience was responsive to every mood of the preacher, and a running commentary was kept up. If the minister said, "You can't do so and so," the response came, "'Course you can't," "The idea, no! no!" "I guess not," "You're right," and similar phrases; while "glory," "hallelujah," "bress de Lord," from the beginning to the end, punctuated almost every sentence of the preacher. Early in the service the "power" began to work. In the prayer we were startled by a most unearthly shriek in the centre of the house. We supposed that some one had been stabbed; but seeing no commotion we thought that perhaps it was a custom of the country, and really, in the excess of negro population, a man or two less did not matter. But shortly after, across the aisle from us there came such a sound as we had never heard; it was a mixture of squeal, shriek, and squawk, in about equal parts. We almost jumped from our seat in fright, turned, and saw a cross-eyed negro girl lying upon the seat, kicking for dear life, with hands clawing in most alarming proximity to us, bonnet off, eyes rolling, body becoming rigid, while with jerky ejaculations, she exclaimed, "Bress de Lord! I got de power." Other sisters were trying to bend her back into shape; but she was enjoying it too much to yield readily to treatment. Even then it did not dawn upon us that this was the common method of negro worship. And while we were wondering whether with the next lurch the power might not land her in our arms, the preacher looked down upon us, and smiling said, "Don't be alarmed; it isn't anything,—she is only happy." It was very assuring, and doubtless stated the condition of her mind; but it did not give adequate description of our feelings. Well, this was only one of many incidents of like character during that eventful service. At its conclusion the collection was in order. The trustees filed into the chancel, and with baskets in hand addressed the audience. Putting the baskets then upon the table, they called for the friends to rally. Meantime the singing was resumed, — the same strange, weird songs, each having a refrain. There was a peculiar, swinging motion to the songs, that made it seem as though, if one should only launch upon them, he could swing to and fro all day.

One particularly had this motion. We could not catch the words, but the beginning of the swing took place on "A dying thief rejoiced;" and with this they swung to and fro. Another really delightful melody was, "I want to be ready when the Bridegroom comes!" As the songs went on, the stragglers, one by one, walked up to the chancel and put in their contributions, the deacons making change in the most business-like manner. The singing waxed warm as the moments flew past; and at last the masterpiece of song was rendered in "Come where the billows roll. I 've been redeemed; I never mean to die no more." The sentiment of the hymn and the chorus-like movement were inspiring. By the time they had got into the middle of it, about the twentieth verse, we found ourselves singing with the rest of them; and at last, in we trust harmonious unison with the defective-eyed girl across the aisle, we ourselves were singing, "Roll, billows, roll," with all the unction if not the music of the best of them. At the conclusion of the hymn, the blackest-looking officer in the group behind the chancel rail exclaimed, "Well, breddren, dem billows roll just beautiful; but I notice dat de nickels ain't rollin' into dese baskets very much. Come, breddren, keep de ark a-movin'. Give us nudder song."

We almost impoverished ourselves in trying to help the deacons out. We sent up our nickels by the children; and every time we made a motion toward our pocket some observant brother would grab a basket and hand it to us. Then the sisters went among the people, and this took another subsidy. The ultimatum was finally given that the service could not be concluded until five more nickels were given, to make even money. The nickel seemed to be the multiple of value. We waited, but no one responding, we took our last quarter and shied it over the chancel rail; and in summing up our donations, we found that the evening service had cost us about the price of a good opera ticket. But then no opera ever gave so much for so small a fee.

The last scene in the service was a baptism. The minister introduced the ordinance with a general scolding on the impropriety of bringing children to be baptized at the evening meeting, and gave emphatic notice that the thing must end. "Well, now," he said, "bring up de baby." The procession started, — a young woman with a child, and an old woman with a boy. With a prefatory sermon on baptism, with a spiteful hit or two at the Baptists, the preacher took the child and sprinkled the water on it. The little one yelled with vigor, when the minister, by way of benediction, shouted, "May dis child grow up to be a good woman, and hate de Debil as it hates water." The charge to the mother was elaborate, for in it he rebuked the sins of the people. He charged her to bring the child to church, and vented his scorn on his people for their dereliction in this regard. On the subject of education he said, "Educate dis child; it better hab only one shirt to its back, and go to bed while it is being washed, dan to grow up wid a head as empty as an old gourd widout any seeds." So he exhorted the mother. Finally, turning to the godmother, he said, "Now, as de godmudder of dis chile, if dis mudder dies, you are to do de tings I hab charged de mudder to do." At this stage from the audience rang out the cry, "She ain't de mudder of dat chile!" "She ain't de mudder of dat chile; who is de mudder of dat chile?" said the preacher. "Dere she is over in dat pew." "Are you de mudder of dis chile? Why don't you come out here? Are you 'shamed to be de mudder of dis chile?" "No, I ain't 'shamed." said a comely woman, as she came out and took her place at the chancel rail. The minister had charged the wrong woman. The evening was getting late; the exhortation could not be repeated; and so with such grace as he could command, he transferred the admonitions. Turning to the boy, he said, "What is de name of dis boy?" "He ain't going to be baptized; he is de godfader," was the answer. "He de godfader!" said the preacher; "he ain't big enough to be a godfader, he doesn't know de obligations. Well, well, it is too late now; but grow up, grow up quick, little godfader, and run to Jesus and get into de kingdom ob heben." So ended the strange christening service.

We can only give it in faintest outline, and cannot picture the surroundings, — the quaintly dressed people, the constant ejaculations, the moving to and fro, the quaintly humorous manner of the preacher, the intent interest of the great assembly. As the meeting dissolved, the elders and preachers gathered round us, while the sisters of the church came up and asked us who we were. We were of course a little flattered, and think that perhaps our fine work on the chorus of the "Roll, billows, roll," had not escaped their notice, though the "other half," as we walked homeward, was mean enough to say, "Don't flatter yourself that it was your singing that gave you the attention of those old women; it was the quarters that you gave that did the business." At any rate, we went to our furnished lodgings with the comforting assurance that when our Northern parish shall put us out, it is probable that the saints of Liberty Street will take us in.

RUNNING THE GAUNTLET OF THE "ISMS."

IT was my misfortune to be born in New England in its era of "isms." I never knew the philosophy of the law by which the star of empire moves westward, but have noticed that epidemics somehow follow the same course, and that the world's "isms" drift from the east in the path of shifting populations. Some writer tells of coming north on the advancing tide of blossoms, travelling with the movement of the season, and reaching every place at the same time as the flowers. I have lived a somewhat migratory life, and have seemed to drift with the "isms." The affliction of a new "ism" upon a community has somehow been coincident with the affliction of my own residence there; and when the delusion has spent its force and passed on to pastures new, somehow I have been breaking camp at the same time.

De Quincey cleverly tells how the traveller's trunk, by the labels which it bears, reveals the progress of his journey; and in the various residences of one who had the misfortune not only to be a minister but a minister's son, and consequently to live always in "the drift period," I can almost to a day date the breaking out of every "ism" that has afflicted the New England and Middle States for the last thirty years.

I came into the world by the way of the Kennebec River, to find the whole down-east population running mad over the "cold-water cure." In almost every house there was built in the breeziest corner of the woodshed, or in the north side of the house, a kind of torture closet, whose floor was perforated for the free passage of the wind, and whose ceiling was covered with a large tin vessel with a kind of watering-pot attachment worked with a string.

The springs of Maine are not thermal. The legend exists that water freezes there the year round, and that the Knickerbocker Company saws ice on the Kennebec during every month.

Well, these perforated pans would be filled with this untempered water; and human beings in whom the love of life was supposed to be strong would with their own hands bring down upon their heads a thousand torturing streams, deluding themselves the while with the thought that this was a panacea for every human ill. In reading from time to time reports of prison management I have noticed that the shower-bath treatment, in the more barbarous States, is in great favor for punishing refractory criminals. It was not possible in large families to keep the children all the time in the shower-bath, but for the little intervals between the pulling of the string, there was the "wet sheet" and the "compress."

I was literally cradled in a bath-tub, and brought up in a shower-bath. My croups were crushed with a compress, and my colds frightened out of me with the horrors of a "wet sheet." I candidly believe that I was cheated out of half the ailments which are esteemed one of the perquisites of childhood by the ever-present spectre of the "cold-water cure."

I have sometimes wondered what I might not have accomplished, if I had not sweated out half my energy in the compresses of my boyhood days, and have always been ready to palliate my shortcomings by asking, "What could be expected of one shaken into the world from a wet sheet; whose brain was flattened in a shower-bath; who was brought up by water-power?" I have been able somewhat to soften my mortification at the humiliations of my native State by the thought that those who are now its arbiters were, a generation ago, the subjects of the cold-water cure. It is not strange that some of its victims should show its effects in the idiocy of later life.

I graduated out of the shower-bath into the age of "Graham,"—a kind of unleavened-bread period, in which men tried to live on sawdust and grow strong by starvation.

The period is not one whose remembrances are kept fresh by frequency of recollection; but the vision that vaguely and indistinctly haunts my mind is that of long-haired men and short-haired women, sallow of face, with lean and hungry looks, like macerated saints, the growth of whose heads was all on the outside.

I wait with impatience the advent of the modern Buckle, who shall give us the philosophy of the law which links together hair and reform. To see the unkempt bangs of a female tramp, or the flowing locks of a masculine interrupter of our peace, is to see a reformer who wishes to convert us to some new delusion, and in the mean time would like to negotiate a temporary loan. If the literalism of art, now so much in vogue, shall continue, the philosophic artist of the future will need to paint Luther with the long hair of Absalom, and to make Garrison a facsimile of the Spartan soldiers whom Xerxes saw combing their tresses in the pass of Thermopylæ.

The Modern Life Insurance Company is now the asylum of those of the clergy who find that they have mistaken their calling, or of whom the church is not worthy; but in the days of my youth, the "isms" furnished inviting shelter. Magnetism, biology, psychology, and all "ologies" save theology had wonderful fascination for these genial visionaries; and when phrenology burst like a meteor on New England, from the ranks of the ministry came forth many apostles of the new gospel of bumps.

In those days the parsonage was a free hotel for the brethren; and my feet were blistered by the errands of the visiting lecturers, while I have always half attributed my fall into public life to my introduction on the platform as a subject in those phrenological days. My wonder has not yet abated at the exceeding volubility of those peripatetic ex-minister lecturers. The little plaster heads were always amusing; and it was doubtless from these things that I got the belief that the brain was a kind of chest of drawers containing each a faculty, and the bumps were a sort of labelled knot which pulled them out. My confidence was greatly shaken when one of these fellows, in going over my head, uttered the alarming prophecy that I should one day be a minister; and so, while I had noticed that it was seldom that any two told the same story, fearing that by some misadventure the dreadful intelligence might be confirmed, I thereafter kept my head out of their hands, though, by compulsion, my legs were still at their disposal.

I had one bump that was a perfect Waterloo for these fellows. They used to build up every imaginable career on the foundation of that innocent protuberance. Delineators of pessimistic tendencies found it the basis of all the crimes, and the sunny optimists saw in it the credentials of my canonization. It never, however, staggered the brethren or failed to receive a name. It was of course a wicked thing to say, but the love of truth was strong with me in those days, and perhaps, too, to please the boys, I used to remark, "That bump is where a horse kicked me when I was six years old," — which was a fact, though by no means to be mentioned in that presence.

I suppose it was largely because I had a kind of constitutional aversion to liquors of every kind that I became zealous in the flourishing temperance organization in the little Cape Ann village, which had never known a drunkard. The precocity of my talents, together with the fact that the lodge of cadets to which I belonged had but few members, early gave me the position of "outside sentinel,"— an office which I subsequently learned was of low rank. My duties were especially fitted to one of active temperament, consisting largely in knocking my heels together outside in the cold, announcing all comers through a knot-hole in the door with a slide over it, and then by a kind of antiphonal knocking, sliding in the brother and leaving myself alone at the head of the windy stairs. We used to meet over an engine-house, just in front of a graveyard, and were "great on receptions," to which we used to invite the girls. The older boys liked it, but it was a kind of bore to us younger ones, because we disliked to ask the girls

and were afraid to come home alone after the receptions were over, and the young misses were set down at their fathers' gates.

We used to wear a kind of white regalia, starched in the upper part, just where it bore upon the neck; were always strong on processions, and looked, I imagine, not greatly unlike the "Ancient Order of Hibernians," who seem to monopolize the parading business in these modern times.

It does not become me to say how much the ravages of the monster Rum were lessened by our parades and picnics; but I have no doubt our work was quite as effectual as much of the more pretentious temperance work of later times.

The "Sugar Pill" epidemic came as a blessed reaction to those who had tortured themselves with hydropathy and starved themselves with Graham grits. I early was taught that homœopathy was the lost Pleiad, the eighth wonder, the philosopher's stone and fountain of youth; that arnica would heal every outward ill, and aconite exorcise every inward ill. I had a vague idea that somehow the future state of those who died under the old-school treatment was hardly as sure as might be desired, while to take the beautiful "similia-similibus" globules of the new school was to inherit the earth and outlive the patriarchs.

It was an improvement on the compress; and the

mastication of a sugar pill, and the cautious smelling of a drop of the fifth reduction of a tincture in a bowl of water, was more to be desired than the felicities of a wet sheet. I was a ready convert; and when the springtime came, and the little pills were substituted for the sulphur and molasses with which I had been wont to hail the flowers, I bore the change with that patient resignation which becomes those whose duty it is to obey.

About this time I emerged from the old home nest; and though I always avoid an argument with the old-school doctors, nevertheless, I take my sugar pills with thankfulness and with what faith I can command, and trust the rest to Providence.

For several years I lived in a community in Massachusetts that was greatly stirred by the Spiritualism that sprang up on the heels of the Rochester Knockings. Come-outer-ism flourished greatly in that region, its disciples, as a rule, refraining from toil through the week, that they might ostentatiously labor upon the Sabbath. In the heart of Vermont, where a part of my school life was passed, I found myself among the Second Adventists,— a quiet, dreamy people, who seemed blighted with the fatal paralysis which this belief somehow seems to bring. I was too young to enter fully into the great strife of abolitionism, but remember well how fervently devoted to this "ism" were those with whom I lived. As a boy I was taken to the great meetings of the day, and young as I was, learned from the lips of Burlingame, Wilson, and others like them, the solemn meaning of the great struggle which was coming on. For years the "Liberator" was read with avidity, and many of those old events, the rendition of Burns and scenes of that kind, come up from early childhood like the phantom of a dream; while not a few of the stirring words of those fateful days come from time to time, sounding out of the far-off past like the rallying blast of a brazen trumpet. In later days, I have become acquainted with the mind cure and faith cure, Christian Science, and those multitudinous other systems which are mainly based on saying you are not sick, and sticking to it, when you know you are. But then, as Rudyard Kipling says, "that is another story."

A SHATTERED DREAM.

I HAD fancied the thing from the start. Even the cumbersome three-wheelers that the boys used, I liked; and when, in the evolutionary process, the nickel-plated, ball-bearing Columbia came, one of the special dreams of a by no means visionary mind was to be the owner of a bicycle and ride up and down the world like other folks. To be sure, I am not quite the spry young fellow I used to be when I was the champion expert on the swings and bars, and pulled the stroke oar in the college boat. But still I am at least forty years away from the cane and crutch, and am vain enough to think that in wind and limb I need ask no odds of the younger generation. I have cherished the delusion, too, that I have quite the form for the saddle-perch of a nickel-plated wheel, and have been so favored by indulgent Nature that I should not suffer with the short-legged trousers of the wheelman's costume.

There was something fascinating in the noiseless glidings of the rubber-tired wheels, while the maximum of speed at a minimum of labor was a condition that delighted. I had been a subscriber to the "Wheelman" from the start, and have fair knowledge of the long distance records. I have been a guest at the annual dinners of the clubs, and have kept my conscience clear at the festivities, with the knowledge that though the speech I made was poor, the fear of making it had saved the victuals of the club. To be a wheelman and wear the shapely stockings was the dream and desire of my heart. But even dreams are subject to amendment; and when one night I picked up the victim of a "header," and helped straighten out his fractured nose, I concluded to add another wheel to the conveyance I would purchase, and would do my summer rambling with an anti-header tricycle instead of bicycle, for this was before the days of the modern "Safety" wheel.

To this complexion had I come, when on my day of disenchantment the small boy of the household came in, and with such insinuating sophistries as the youngsters have when they have an axe to grind and wish the parental hand upon the crank, suggested that sire and son should take a turn, simply as a kind of breathing matter and to test the motion of the wheel. As I look back upon it now, I remember that I was somewhat muddled in the handling of the prophecy that was the subject of the morning's sermon; and more to get rid of interruption than because of desire to make an exhibition, I gave consent, making stipulation that the place of my assignation with the wheel should be beyond the limits of the ward.

In a jaunty making-call kind of walk, I sauntered down to the place of rendezvous; and while the nimble-footed heir went back for his own three-wheeler, I bent the forces of my intellect to studying the secrets of the craft that was to carry me. It had two wheels with bulging spokes, with a kind of annex following after wheel which was the rudder. Endless chains, like those which brought up the water twenty years ago in the New England wells, went round a kind of drum which had attachment with the treadles; and though I had never ridden the thing, nor even sat upon it, my native sense suggested that I had only to put my feet upon the cranks and "let nature work," and I should go spinning round the world. There were ivory-handled things which worked the steering gear, and lots of places where the oil ran out, making confidences with my clothes.

Another lad had joined us; and in nonchalant manner I mounted. It seemed easy to get on, catch hold, fish up the treadles, and churn away with ease and confidence. I had the theory to perfection, but from the start lacked executive power. The treadles got away from me, and the steering apparatus missed connection and landed me against a lamp-post. The thing did not start as if it had any heart in the business; and though the small boy dismounted and lent a pushing hand, it was not the easy thing I had imagined to keep the circulation up. I am still of the opinion that the fine young fellows who work these monsters with such deceptive grace have passed some years in a treadmill, and that no one who has not served the State in that capacity can attain either speed or admiration on a three-wheeler. In a laborious life I have had hard tasks; but could the lower muscles speak, I am certain they would say they found that day their hardest task. Somehow I could not get the double action of the thing. I could make it go, but I could not make it steer; or if I could steer it, I could not make it go. Having to make a choice, I took motion rather than grace, and went ricochetting down the avenue, the terror of pedestrians. More than once I narrowly escaped entanglement with carriage-wheels; horses shied at me; coachmen raised their voices and would have used their whips save for the something in my eye that said I was not in trifling mood. The power left me on the track of an advancing car, and I should have abandoned the thing then and there, had the getting off been simply a matter of the will. I was half the time butting against the curb, although I treated both sides of the street with generous impartiality. So I made my journey, working with such vehemence that the perspiration covered me, though it was an autumnal day and those who were riding were hugging their furs about their shivering forms.

I could have stood the work, for I am not accounted lazy, but a heavier cross was laid upon me. I did not actually know, but I surmised, that the whole city went out that day for an airing on the road that I had taken. I can of course now recall friends that did not pass me on the way, but they are few. My congregation, certainly, by some prearrangement was out in force. Almost before I had learned the rudder's larboard and starboard side, I saw one of the broad-aisle fellows bearing down on me. He had his daughter with him, the veriest laughter-loving tease in the church; and should she spy me, the day would be a long way off when she would forget the apparition, and the conversation would be wonderfully compact that would not afford a gap by which the story of my discomfiture would be introduced. They did not see me at the first; and because I dared not abandon the machine and run and hide as I would have liked to do, I got off, grabbed a wrench, and doubling myself up, with back toward the advancing carriage, pretended that I was tightening some imaginary bolt. It was a dead failure; the carriage stopped; pleasant laughter rippled toward me. I hammered at the bolt but gave no sign, but it was without avail. I turned my crimson face and sought excuses, in that I was doing it to please the boy; extended my repairs, hoping that they would shorten their visit, but they waited to see the mount, and I shall never be grateful enough to the good fortune that enabled me to catch the treadles and get away with a fair amount of grace.

I saw everybody but the small boy whom I was looking for to take the thing home. People whom I had never spoken to nodded from their cushions; ladies in their carriages put their heads from their windows and called me by my name; children in the Sunday-school ran up to see just how the parson did it, that they might give report in the to-morrow's classes; and I am half confident I never saw in so short a time so many friends, and fully certain that I never wished to see them less. I had come the whole distance under protest. The boys had persuaded me, and to coax me on had said, even when the pedals stuck and I was bumping against the curb, that I was doing beautifully; although when they had wheeled a block or so ahead I could see the rascals' shaking sides, and knew that they were laughing at me. Had I been governed by my better judgment I should have sent the thing home, though I had had to pawn my watch and take passage in the cars.

Well, to close the chapter of misadventures, I had come to the hill that stretches to the boulevard by the prison. The tug was hard, because the grade was steep. The small-boy nuisance abounded now upon the sidewalk, insisting on giving aid for a consideration. I knew, though I was working with desperation, that it would never do to have the friends who were bowing kindly at me see me being pushed along by half a score of dirty boys; and though I would not have begrudged the money if I could have had the "push," my self-respect compelled refusal, though I was aching in every joint. The boys somehow knew that I wanted them, and so they tagged behind; while one, more cruel than the rest, cried out, "Oh, see the dude!" which of all the horrors of that afternoon was the unkindest cut. The top of the hill was reached; I turned homeward, and was ready for the start, when gently coming on me was the span of another pew-holder, who from below had spied his friend and hurried up to pass the time of day. He knew that I was not a happy man, although the dream of home and the down-grade before me had somewhat raised my spirits. Thanks to the law of gravitation, the first stage of the homeward way would be easy. I got on, and she started; the brake would not work and I did not care; the horses shied, but that was not my affair; the small boys jeered, but I was homeward bound, and until the chain broke I had the first real enjoyment of the day. I got off and went back and got the chain. The curious crowd began to gather; a couple of riders, whom I had never seen, stopped, and calling me by name offered to assist; and while the tinkering went on, being tendered the machine that one of my companions rode, I mounted that and rode away, leaving him to get back the broken one as best he could. The grade was easier, and I was getting the motion now, while the borrowed machine had the steering wheel ahead, which helped me some; and so, led on by that "vaulting ambition which o'erleaps itself," I tried to speed the thing. I knew not how it happened, but perhaps I was driving it a little hard; at any rate, suddenly the chain of this one snapped, and I was left beside the road with a second wreck upon my hands.

The boys were behind towing the other ruin, there were no more worlds to conquer or machines to break, so gathering up the greasy chain and hiring, at most usurious rates, a small boy to push it home, and subsidizing another boy to go with him for company, I started homeward the procession of broken-downs; while with hands and coat soiled with grease and dust, I walked back good two miles, laughing to myself, as I watched the boys, that I had gained deliverance at such easy price as the rebuilding of the wrecks and the pensioning of the boys.

I would remark, in closing these confessions, that for several years I was not the enthusiastic wheelman that I had been when cycling with me was a theory rather than a condition. But with the coming of the Safety, and the healing of my wounds, I have pieced together the fragments of my shattered dream, and am in competition for the biggest medal of the city club.

"WHITE WINGS."

THERE are some positions in which a man finds himself that require explanations. The ownership of a yacht by a poor man and a sane man, a man, too, who has no instinct of sailorship, whose head always turns with the lifting of the first wave, is such a situation. Our record is against us too, for we have spent our life in declaiming against the dangers of the fatal sail; and as if to make our later humiliation all complete, we issued orders not a week ago to the young scion who will be the heir of our liabilities and compromise with our creditors, that on no account should he during the summer venture his foot in a boat with sail. And there she lies on this peaceful morning not three hundred feet away. For an hour at least, the line by which she rides at anchor has hung limp, so motionless are the waters. There is a double picture everywhere. Each tree has another self within the water, and every cloud has a reflected cloud looking upward from the river. The Revelator's sea of glass was not more still and rippleless than is this fair St. Lawrence on this summer's morning.

Such is the day on which "White Wings" rides at anchor. Had we been long the owner of her, she might not seem so beautiful; but now her lines are fair, and with a thousand graces she lifts her mast against the background of the sky, — the fairest vision amid all the glories of this enchanted morning.

Well, it is a long story, for we come to our larger follies by degrees. The boys did it. They entrapped us into a neighbor's boat as a kind of ballast; and we went, that their safety might be insured. The intoxication of the dancing waves got hold of us. The grandfather of one of the conspirators was then invited, and caught the epidemic, and we became fools together. The women laughed at us, but an hour's sail against the wind made them pleaders for the boys. Of course it has been awkward to explain some past remarks, and it has taken some sharp turnings to show that we have been quite consistent. But we hold the power of invitation in our hands; and if the tormenting becomes too severe, we can omit the offenders from the list of those who are asked to share our voyages.

And then it was such a bargain; and there were two of us. Why, a few less bonnets for the wives, the old feathers recurled instead of cast away, a few less dresses, — and the thing is paid for. We have ciphered it out, and know that the expenditure was wise. Of course there are some things we did not think of. The seller of the boat was a little over-sanguine in saying that the sails were good for half-a-dozen years; they will have to be replaced next season. An anchor must be procured at once; the cabinet-work be repaired. The skiff we crushed at our neighbor's dock, after the seller left us with his check, was not repaired for half the estimate he put upon the job; and the dismantling and outfitting and the winter's care we find are items which were not considered when we felicitated ourselves upon being the owners of a yacht.

But there she rides at anchor; and if she never left her moorings she is worth all she cost, or most of it, for the picture she makes on the enchanted waters of this summer's morning. However, she is not to ride at anchor thus. Within our veins is yet the thrill of yesterday's excitements. How splendidly she sailed! We were certain that nothing on these waters could outsail her, until the "Water Witch" came out and marched right by us on the windward side. We are not skilful yet in all the science of sailorship. Our partner will have to stop speaking of the "downhill" and "uphill" sides, and use leeward and windward; and when we tell him again to "luff her up," he must not stop and ask us what we mean by luffing her. But then we know more than we used to know. We know that it is not safe to take a standing jibe, and that in tacking we must bring her in the wind; that the rope which holds the long pole at the bottom of the sail must not be tied; that the clothes-lines which hoist the sail must not be tangled; and that a boat with a five-foot draught cannot go over a two-foot shoal. Of course this is not much, but it is a good deal more than we knew a week ago.

Well, we never knew till now what we missed in our yachtless days, — the exhilaration, the sense of mastery, the freshness and splendor of the air, the sense of motion. New worlds have opened to us; and the fair scenery of these islands, the splendid reaches of these incomparable waters, have a double charm now that we can explore them on the wings of the wind. What cruises we will take, what visions we will have, what music will come from dashing sprays, what friendships will we make, as we sit beneath our sails and are borne hither and thither by "White Wings" in the days that are to be!

SORRENTO.

THERE is no vision on the earth more fair than the Bay of Naples from the heights of St. Elmo. The city reveals only its beauty, hiding its deformity; the sea is blue and radiant with the light that glorifies it; and the magic circlet of the shore that bounds it is made of fair cities that have historic fame. In the distance, fair Capri rises empurpled from the sea, and Ischia and other islands add romance and beauty to the fairest panorama the earth contains. The line of smoke floats like a black plume from the distant steamers, while fishers' boats with lateen sails are in the nearer vision, like painted ships upon a painted sea. The days at Naples are revelations, and at night the soul is awed with a beauty that seems to be not of earth.

Vesuvius, with its faint cloud of smoke rising like an exhalation, sits like a monarch in the midst of splendors; and cities, towns, and vineyards, fields over which historic armies have marched, heights and headlands on which poets have sat and sung immortal songs, make up the details in the fair picture that one sees, as from St. Elmo's heights he looks down upon the enchanted bay and the fair shores that are kissed by its waters.

Leave behind the tenantless streets of Pompeii, and ride along the shore to fair Sorrento, and nowhere shall you find a road more wondrous. Following every indentation of the coast, winding along the borders of every cliff, the road is a path of fair surprises, opening at every headland fairer outlooks, and at every landward turn revealing vistas of field and forest. Now far below the waters break in surging monotones against the base of beetling crags; the draperies of sea-weed floating in and out with the pulsing of the waves; and then the road drops down, until the wheels traverse the white beaches of the sea. Up again and on, winding amid cliffs and crags, the road goes on; inward by rocky vine-clad gorge, terraced with olive-trees, the road gives glimpses of white villas peeping from the darker foliage of the fig and orange trees. Between the cliffs there are sheltered coves, with tiny boats upon their beaches, and bathers sporting in the waves. The villages are quaint, with curious houses painted with the brilliant colors that these sunny-hearted Italians love, with wayside shrines consecrated to the Holy Virgin, with faded flowers which love or penitence has offered with a prayer. In the tiny shops and on the sidewalk the little industries are carried on, and from the balconies black-eyed girls fling down their chattering smiles. So, through Castellamare and other towns, the road comes to fair Sorrento.

It is the place which Nature made for the abiding of those who love her most; and hither they have

come, — poets, to sit upon her cliffs and weave the beauty of her scenes into verse; artists, who have tried, but tried in vain, to paint some of the visions splendid; novelists, to make this the place of their romances; and lovers, to add the witcheries of her enchantments to their tales of love.

Backward toward the mountains there are winding roads, shadowed with fair forests, peasants' homes set in the midst of orchards garlanded with vines; and on the seaward side, the great cliff rises, and on the rim of it Sorrento sits, as kings and poets have sat on these cliffs on summer days and looked out on the sea. You shall find no hotel in Europe more finely placed than the Tramontane at Sorrento. Drop a stone from the balcony of its upper rooms, it shall go down three hundred feet to the very beach on which the Italian fishermen and women are chanting their songs as they draw their nets. On the sea are fisher-boats with curiously fashioned and colored sails. The water is so clear that one can note the shells on the bottom of the sea. Go, by winding subterranean passages, to the beach below. Swim in the waters of this Bay of Naples, with all the tides of the Mediterranean lifting you in their mighty arms. The delicious waters fold you with a caress, and the tonic of the salt sea gives the invigoration of youth to every nerve. Then come back, and from the upper balcony look out on Nature's masterpiece. There is the reddening glow of sunset in the west. Look straight across; that whitened cliff rising from the sea is Ischia, and with a narrow belt of sea between, the adjacent cliff is the northern horn of the crescent that makes the incomparable bay. In high-sloping hills, the line of coast comes on, rimmed with fair cities, reaching upward through orchard-girdled towns, until the summit of Vesuvius is reached. This is the line that is set against the horizon. How fair Naples is, behind the veil of distance that is between it and

Sorrento! Its beggar's rags are changed to a monarch's royal robes; and from its beaches to its summit, where is the castle of St. Elmo and the monastery of St. Martino, there is no sign of anything that is not beautiful.

In the little bay beyond lies Castellamare, and behind it are its mountains, set as foothills against the background of the Apennines. These things are only the dotted outlines of the picture of Naples and its environs, as seen from the cliff at Sorrento; to complete the picture one must put in a multitude of villages, with groves and terraced hills, winding paths, villas, and monasteries, the ruins of old castles with the ever-changing panorama of the sea, and the matchless canopy of an Italian sky.

Wander where one will, he cannot err in this delicious region; every path is fit for a lovers' walk, and every headland for a poet's musings. The peasants' cottages, the fishers' villages in the tiny coves below, the winding paths which find the summits of the hills, the old houses where the world's poets lived and wrote the songs which the world for centuries has sung, — everything at fair Sorrento touches the heart with the spell of romance and beauty. Life becomes idyllic; and the heart is tenanted with memories which will last through the eternities.

But Sorrento is the city of the sea, rather than of the land. It never can escape allegiance to the siren sea, that holds it captive with a thousand fascinations. Is there any sea so blue? Is there elsewhere on any waters such varied life? Has any bay a tithe of the splendor that rims around the Bay of Naples, as seen from Sorrento, with its islands and its cities? — Naples a magic city by day, a crescent of fire by night, while Vesuvius, by day a pillar of cloud, by night a pillar of fire, sentinels the glorious scene.

Every hour of the day brings a new transformation in the shifting kaleidoscope of beauty. The day comes to the songs of the fishermen drawing their nets beneath Sorrento's cliffs; at noonday the sea becomes rippleless, and Naples changes from a city to a mirage; and when the night comes on, and one by one the lights go out that make the towns and cities a coronal of fire around the bay, then within the hospitable walls of the Tramontane there are the peasants dancing the Tarantella to the pleasant music of the castanets, — and then sleep and its dreams, but never can the dreams of night or day be half so fair as the realities of the Bay of Naples and fair Sorrento.

A LOST ART.

CALLING upon a friend upon a winter's night, we found him sitting by his study fire, reading the letters of his grandmother, written nearly a hundred years before. They were yellow with age, written in curiously fashioned characters, and bearing the marks that age inflicts.

Her home was in New England; and in these silent chronicles there were many pictures of the rude life of those early days. The villages were far apart, and through the woods she used to ride on visitations to her friends. Life was simple in its necessities, and there was little movement or color in its unfoldings. The stir of cities spent its noise long before it could reach the quiet Berkshire region where she lived, and the great outward world that beat its measures on the borders of the sea seemed like a fairy world, so far was it away.

The letters were written in what must have been her middle life, for they contained the story of her household cares, and were full of tender apprehension for the boy she loved.

He had gone through the wilderness, seeking fortune in the mysterious city, and these letters were fragrant with the prayerful followings of her mother-love. She was a child of the Puritans, and had a religious faith which glowed in all the unconscious utterances of these letters of friendship. And yet she lived far enough away from the sterner age of faith to have love for Nature and the graces of humanity; and though she felt the reality of faith, it was something tender and alluring, and worship was joy, and devotion rapture.

She described the Sabbaths as they passed, and how the birds sang to her as she walked to service through the woods, and how the silence of the Sabbath brooded over her like a dream of heaven, and how she gathered with the saints, and in the silence of her meditation mingled loving memories of the absent boy with her prayers to God. She told the story of the preacher's words; and though the sermon was of the sterner cast that marked the olden days, yet in passing through her mind it had caught a grace which changed it almost into a poet's idyl. There was no hint of petty gossip, nor the pardonable frivolity which even the souls of saints are wont to witness when they touch for a time the vanities of a world of fashion; but the memories of the Sabbath were of prayer and song, the meditations of the house of God, which was the gate of heaven. It was only a glance into the sacred sanctuary of a woman's heart that had turned to dust half a century ago; but it revealed a life as sweet as the lives of saints, and brought vision of such living as poets sing of, where life's hard conditions are changed into content and radiance by the alchemy of a faith that can transmute common things into heroic life.

The story of these faded letters suggests the query whether the letter-writing of the past is not a lost art. Is there anywhere in New England now one single saint who makes, in the confidence of friendship, such chronicles of her daily life? Who tells how the days come and what they bring, what moods of thought, what hopes and fears? Who breathes in language her silent prayers, and lets her inmost heart tell the story of its joys and griefs?

The world's literature has nothing equal in revelation to the letters that have been written from heart to heart, without one thought that the world would ever read; and to-day, though the world is filled with books, yet the best literature that men have written has never seen the light, for in friendship's letters it has been read and gathered beneath the eaves of garret roofs, or exhaled its riches in the ashes of fires long since burned out.

The letters of Shelley have come down to us, and surely the poet's pen never framed sweeter music than some of the phrases which friendship's wand evoked.

Mesdames de Staël and Récamier conquered the social world by the sovereignty of the pen. Nowhere does Thackeray so reveal his inner life as in the unconscious utterances of the letters of personal friendship. In his public works there is the taint of cynicism; but when heart speaks to heart, there is the genuine ring of a soul that cries exultantly, "God lives; all's well with the world!" We saw a letter once written by the Adams who was known by his generation as the man of controversy and war; and yet here in the letter there was revealed the sunny side of the great man's nature, and there was grace and tenderness, a touch of poetry even, and such kindliness for all the world as no one could even dream belonged to the stern man of war and battle.

The plays of Shakespeare reveal all the secrets of all men's minds, save that of Shakespeare's own. They contain all revelations save self-revealings; for the king of art, obedient to the laws of his own sovereign realm, concealed the creator's personality behind the created things. What would the world not give if only it could somewhere find that precious bundle of faded letters sent from London to the little home at Stratford, where Anne Hathaway lived and waited for the coming back of the absent one, until at last, with fortune won, they should come together to their "Castle in Spain," beside the reeds and rushes of the gentle Avon? What rare wit, what sweet philosophy, would be found in the letters of the absent husband to his wife, written in the midst of his creative inspirations, brilliant with the glow of his divinest moods; or when, the immortal work finished, the poet's hand, made clever with its facile workings, strung on the golden thread of love the jewels which, because of the richness of his treasures, he could not use in weaving the embroideries of kings.

The French cynic used to say that the object of language was to conceal thought; but when men talk as the birds sing to their solitary mates, when mothers talk to children over the wastes of distance, when hearts use that secret language which, like the cipher speech of ambassadors to kings, is known only to the one addressed, then language is not a mask, but an interpreter. There is no literature, save the literature of written letters, where such language can be used; there is no writing, save that of personal letters, which can be free from the self-consciousness which makes men hypocrites; and the world is the loser, and falsehood gains, when the pen of friendship loses the art of speech, and the secrets of human hearts can find no language with which to tell their tale.

The uncovering of the tombs of Deirel-Bahari have brought to light the bodies of the Egyptian kings who ruled when Israel was in bondage. The mummy-cloths tell the story of the Pharaohs and bring back the very dynasties which saw the birth of the world's most fateful nation. So there are hidden somewhere, in forgotten letters, dynasties of genius, words which, could they only come to light, would sway imagination and be the seed-thoughts of new creations. The story of our war thus slumbers yet, as the seven sleepers slept. It has never been told, nor will it, until from the thousand attics of New England and Western homes, from the old boxes beneath the eaves, from the old chests, where in neglect and forgetfulness they yellow with the years, the letters of the soldier boys are resurrected and made to tell the story of a nation's deliverance. Our printed histories tell only the line of armies' marches, the place of battle, the number slain upon the field, the proclamations of the leaders, the rise and fall of great captains of war. But the nation was saved not by proclamations, but by men; not by leaders and commanders of the people, but by the common soldiers. And how the soldiers' hearts were kept true and loyal, and their courage strong by memories of home; and how electric deeds were stimulated by loving hearts reaching from the homestead to the camp, — this story is told only in the nameless letters, which to-day, wearing still the postmark of the camp, lie neglected and forgotten in a hundred thousand homes.

As we write these random thoughts, we take from their hiding-place some letters that we cherish, and here are the delicate, finely written lines of Chapin; and who would have ever thought that one who wielded the hammer of a Thor, and hurled the lightnings of forceful speech as Jupiter threw his thunderbolts, should have held the pen, which in his grasp was a wizard's wand of power, with a touch as light as that of a woman's hand?

And here is a memento of the great preacher of the ages, with curvatures of line and letter graceful as the fashion of his speech, and in the words a gleam of the humor's sunshine that made Beecher the idolized of men. And here, again, is a letter of the poet, Bayard Taylor, without one hint of the abandon of the poet's touch, but clear and regular, as though written by one whose trade it was to set copies for a school-boy's task. So we might go on and on, and speak of letters as revealers of men, and call forth the forgotten histories that are wrapped within friendship's common letters.

But these things are of the past, for letter-writing is swiftly becoming a lost art. A new age has come, — an age not of confidences, but of business. Trade has annihilated friendship; and the telegraph and postal-card have made obsolete the old-time letters of other days. Letters are bred of sentiment, and sentiment is not in fashion in this age of ours. Emotion is unmannerly; and the god of silence has deposed the deity of confidence. Jerusalem is lighted with incandescent loops, and the tramways will soon be built on the Damascus road. There are no Abrahams now. "What would you do, Tom, if you should receive a message commanding you to offer up your son upon the altar?" "Well," said Tom, who was once a telegraph operator, "I should ask to have the message repeated."

The mail-trains carry heavier freightage than used to go in the pouches of the carrier or the box of the tri-weekly stage; but there was more sentiment and genuine friendship in the saddle-bags of the mail-carrier a century ago than rides now in the postal-cars of the "Chicago specials" or the mail-sacks of the "Shore Line."

Business has no hour in its calendar of duties for friendship, and there is no writing-paper in modern homes, except the pads of the shop. The letter-writer, who could fill his four and forty pages without one hint of shop or market, went out when the telegraph came in, and is now only the fossil of an extinct age. But with his going went one of the best elements of literature, and from the hour of his departure history has been able to fashion only lying chronicles. The lost art of letter-writing is to be lamented not simply for itself alone, but because it indicates that friendship itself is becoming a lost art. "Friendship's affections," Sterne tells us, "are drawn together by fine-spun threads;" and the old saw has it that "A letter timely writ, is a rivet in affection's chain." Napoleon was not a man of friendships, but he knew that a silent absence breeds alienation and forgetfulness, and so he wrote to those he loved, "Let us record the deeds that we have performed together." Let us not deceive ourselves; if friends are forgotten it is because friendship is dead; if after absent friends the heart sends out no following tendrils, it is not because the competitions of a busy age forbid, but because love has such shallow roots that it cannot survive departure. So long as friendship has any vitality of life, it has a language which utters itself across the wastes of space, and by the vehicle of letters, bridges absence and keeps alive its holy fellowships. Absence brings not forgetfulness, for,—

> "Love reckons hours for months and days for years;
> And every little absence is an age."

The admonition of this homily is simply this, that the old-time fashion of our fathers be renewed again; that we pause in the hot racings of our life to foster the friendships of the present and keep alive the loves of other days; that we mingle with the terse letters of our shops those other letters that have no mission other than that of love, and by the written language of friendly letters weave new strands to bind together our forgetful hearts. Some one has said,

"Know, if you have a friend, you ought to visit him often. The road is grown over with grass, the bushes quickly spread over it, if it is not constantly travelled."

The friendly letter is the carrier which keeps hearts in true alliance, and when hearts lose the language of affection love is dumb because it is dead. The world has lost many of the arts it once had learned, but it could better lose all that it has or ever had than to lose the art of all the arts, — the art of friendship.

THE SPRING CLEANING.

I HAVE always asserted that a woman likes house-cleaning with an intensity of affection only inferior to her passion for shopping. The man willing to challenge the truth of the statement never has been found. The feminine instinct for house-cleaning reconciles one to the idea that Adam fell at the suggestion of his wife, and that a certain degree of natural depravity has never been civilized out of the fairer sex.

The periodical ordeal is nearly finished with us, although while this writing is in progress I hear sweet symphonies of the scrubbing-brush on the study door. The smell of soap is rapidly disappearing; and in time, I suppose, the misplaced things will be found, and we shall become reconciled to the loss of the keepsakes that have been destroyed. I console myself with the reflection that it is a sad world anyway, and that my neighbors across the way are now catching the same punishment. My books have been disturbed, my study has been invaded, and life generally made miserable. The cleaners have driven me at the point of the scrubbing-brush from room to room; and writing which began on the lower planes has been finished on the attic heights.

I do not think that there has been in my treatment any special malignity beyond that which is incidental to the natural riot of the cleaning, although I have been careful not to make this admission within my own home. But no way has yet been found by which a woman can clean a house with a man in it with any comfort to the man. I have my own notions of how things will go when the full suffrage comes, and the woman becomes the breadwinner and the man the bread-maker. I shall let the thing go till the house becomes untenantable, and then burn the house.

I have, however, reduced the house-cleaning torture to a minimum, for I have found, in the cellar of a building on a neighboring avenue, a saturnine mechanic, who has rare skill in adjusting carpets, easing doors, mending window-cords, and patching furniture; and by throwing myself back on a personal incompetency, which is largely assumed, this general utility man has gradually usurped my place as a general repairer of the household.

At a heavy cost of personal humiliation I have worked out a philosophy from which I argue that there is nothing more disastrous to a person than to be understood to possess a kind of omniscience. Into the lap of the skilful mender are thrown the undarned stockings of the family; and if only one is content to be thought a fool, he can barter his pride for a vast amount of comfort. The old academy and college chum does not dream to this day that any amount of teaching would ever enable me to build a fire; and I shall never cease to have reproaches for not more generally availing myself of the assumption of a general incompetency.

I have always remembered the beatific joy with which a certain woman once rushed into my presence and exclaimed, "I'm a widow; I'm a widow!" I saw something of this in the good lady who comes round at the semi-annual cleaning and lends a hand. In the gossip of the scrubbers, the infelicities of the sterner sex were commented on, after the pleasant manner that women have. The good woman, with marvellous self-complacency, remarked, "Thank

Heaven! I have no worry about my husband. He is 'sent up' regularly twice a year for six months, and so long as liquor is sold I'll never have to worry as to where he keeps himself nights." In a life of many cares she felt grateful that her lot was not without its pleasant features.

So by working together, we have come to the end of the semi-annual tumult. By careful watching, I have managed to save most of my best clothes from being bestowed on carpet-beaters and scrubbers. The bulk of the library is on the shelves, and the lost sermons and addresses will doubtless be found during the coming season. I have poulticed out the major part of the throat inflammations contracted by the evaporation of the suds, and shall enjoy life with such subdued comfort as is permitted to those who know that there will be another invasion of the scrubbing-pail in the early autumn. I shall be reminded that I have escaped from the spring cleaning as I see my old pantaloons from time to time on the overgrown boys of the artists who served us during the celebration. In the joyfulness of my deliverance, I shall permit my wounds to heal, and forgive, as I have ever done, the tormentors of my peace.

A DREAM OF THE ADRIATIC.

OUR stay in Florence had been brief. The day was hot as no others of the summer were. Our memory of it is of a fair city simmering beside the waters of the yellow Arno, with pleasant morning rides by winding ways to the heights of San Miniato, and delicious loiterings in the shadow of Giotto's princely tower, and the monastery of St. Marco rich with memories of Fra Angelico and Savonarola. But the hot breath of the sirocco was in the air, and we must needs creep within the shadows of the palaces as we walked the streets; and we were glad, yet sad, when we came out of the hot valley of the Arno and wended our way to Venice. Twenty years before we had visited the city. The memory of it had never left us; the music of its waters, the beauty of its palaces, the incomparable grace that makes it the world's wonder city, — all had been cherished; and we came as a lover comes to his beloved, with the rapture of anticipated joy.

And not an expectation was unrealized. Day by day the wonder grew: fair as a dream seemed its palaces; and the magic colors which made every vision an enchanted one never faded into the light of common day. It is not possible for the inartistic mind to see in St. Mark's all the beauty that inspired the pen of Ruskin to its rhapsodies. It does not awe as does the cathedral of Cologne or any of the Gothic structures of the north. Indeed, no architecture save the Gothic gives the soul the thrill of great upliftings. Before the majesty of Milan one stands awed and silent. One feels before that matchless building that out of the perfection of beauty God shines, and strength and beauty are married in the magnificent amplitudes and loveliness of that miracle of marble. There is no such thrill of great emotions before St. Mark's; but it charms and fascinates, it weaves the witchery of its beauty over every sense, and one loves it and comes and looks at it, and comes again and leaves it at last with such a delicious sadness as lovers have at parting.

Venice is old and decayed. It has not rocked the cradle of a single son of commanding fame. It makes merchandise of its beauty and lives upon its memories. It is without industry; there is no thrill of commerce along its water-ways. It is a show city of the past. but Rome is not richer in associations, and no city in the world has a tithe of its unique and bewildering beauty. One never tires of the palaces of the Grand Canal; and in the by-ways, everywhere, there are surprises of loveliness, — a shapely bridge, a façade which combines Grecian form and Oriental color, a distant vista of mingling sky and sea, a graceful tower, a swelling dome, a gondola gliding noiselessly upon the waters like the flitting of a bird, such bewilderment of beauty as makes Venetian days dream-like and unreal.

Nothing in Venice so enraptured as the colors. What it is, — whether some witchery of the air, some alchemy of the sea and atmosphere, or some rare magic of ochre or pigment, — one cannot tell, but the colors had a softness and delicacy indescribable. And the mantle of color was over everything. The Ducal Palace was not marble, but ivory; the palaces of the canals, made of marble, porphyry, and serpentine, were softly hued with rose and pink, and every richness of delicious hues. The very lateen sails of the fishing-boats were dyed with coarse and uncostly colors, but even their homely serviceableness had a softness of hue, as though some fairy goddess had dissolved a jewel in the dyer's vat.

Sitting in the little steamer at the Lido one day, we cast our eyes toward the south and west, and the vision was a kaleidoscope of color, except that the colors of the kaleidoscope are harsh and cold, and these were soft as the mist. We took pencil and paper and drew rough color-sketches of the old walls, the factories, the bit of green before the monastery, the distant islands, trees, clouds, and the lagoon; and then we counted the distinct hues, and there were upward of thirty in the scene swept by our vision. So was it everywhere in Venice. Everything was glorified. The iron buoy floating in the harbor, to which the cables of the Italian iron-clads were fastened, was but a floating iron cask like others of its kind. It was painted red, with good, plain, homely color we have no doubt; but some magic brush had touched it, and its hues were such as Titian might have taken for the Doge's robes within the palace, — soft, a mingled red and rose, so that as it floated there on the surface of the waters it seemed as if it were a rose-leaf set in the foreground of enchanted palaces. Different cities have different colors. Black and white fitly represent Rome, for the old city is colorless. Fiesole and the Arno at Florence need a touch of color, and sunny Naples is a dream of it; but beyond these, plain, uncolored pictures fitly represent the other cities. But Venice uncolored is not Venice. As well portray the frescos of Versailles or the pictures of Titian and Rubens with lights and shades as to picture Venice without the magic colors that are as much a part of her architecture as the columns of her façades and the swelling domes of her churches.

Before the harbor of Venice is the great bar which guards its entrance, and is called the Lido. It is fairly desolate, being only a ridge of sand flecked with trees. There are burial-places on it, buildings not many, tiny villages, a scattered suburban life. But beyond it on the other side is the Adriatic; and here we came, on that first day in Venice, to the great pavilion, to bathe in the waters of that fair sea of which we had dreamed since childhood.

All the way from Florence we had seen the quivering of the olive leaves in the hot sun; the old cities along the way were slumbering in the intensity of heat; the fields were deserted by the peasants; and Venice, which we had left behind, was asleep in the siesta which the heat had made day long. The tourists of the world were here, sitting in the great pavilion above the waters, looking out on the fair sea, while music added its enchantment, and sky and sea mingled in a dream of beauty. There beyond were the coasts of Dalmatia, and beyond the clouds lay Greece.

We had bathed in the Mediterranean at Sorrento, and had felt the splendid thrill of its tonic waters; but when we descended from the pavilion into the shallow waters of the Adriatic, and walked out over the softest sand into the deepening waters until they wrapped us all around, then we felt for the first time the luxury that the sea has when it is rightly attempered to the human frame. The temperature of air and water were almost the same; and something of the softness of the air was in the water, and there was a caressing in its touch, and a soft deliciousness that made life exhilarant, not with any stimulus but by very sensuousness of luxury. And so the moments lengthened, and an hour passed; and with every sense enraptured we came reluctantly out of the sea and went to our home. Every day we went thither; every day the joy was repeated and intensified. Life found renewal in the sea; and while the body was wrapped in the satin folds of the sea, the ear was charmed with the music, and the vision was enthralled with the panorama, of waters. The fishing-boats, gay with their lateen sails, were in the distance; far away were larger vessels, sailing southward, as in the days of the Venetian Doges the ships of the city sailed to Greece and Corinth, every sailor enjoined by edict to bring back some spoil of art or beauty for the enrichment of the city. It was not hard to remember that it was in these very waters that the Bucentaur sailed, and that here the Doge with ring of gold married the sea to Venice as its bride. One day while here, the clouds grew dark and in great wild volumes rolled together in the south, shot through with rays of sunlight, illuminated, permeated with the light, until their blackness changed to purple and amethyst and softest rose, and then, conquered by the light, they melted away into a great sun mist which was like an atmosphere of gold.

Rejuvenated, elate with quickened senses, every breath a joy, and every step a delight, day by day we came back to Venice, by the iron-clads lying at anchor here, by the arsenal from which crusading hosts went forth in other days, with funeral barges slowly guided seaward to the Lido, by fair tourists singing songs of joy, while dome, spire, palace front, and all the bewilderment and grace of beauty were hued in the enchantments of the dying day. Oh, how wonderful it was, and what magic glamours the mingling sea and air can bring here in this fair city by the sea! Then the Venetian nights!—in the piazza with the background of the cathedral and the famed horses of St. Mark's, and the piazzetta with the twin columns which sentinel the waters, and the Ducal Palace, which at night became with its ivory softness a palace of enchantment, and the driftings beneath the Rialto, and by the house of Desdemona, over the waters which had floated armies whose deeds are historic! Then the music at night upon the canals, while the light streamed down from the palaces, and shimmered in the rippling waters; and the long walks through the narrow streets to the little square where Antonio and Bassanio trafficked, crossing the tiny bridges which spanned the dark waters, and seeing the weird shadows of the sombre water-ways!

It may be that one does not feel the awe of great memories in Venice as he does in Rome, nor yet the thrill of great upliftings as at Chamouni looking at the silver peak of Mont Blanc, or any new thrill of liberty as at Geneva, or any quiet reverence for art as at Florence, but for days of dreaming and nights of delicious revery there is no spot like Venice. When the journey is over and one is set again to the hard tasks of life, in those idling moments when the mind is untethered and told to wander where it will, how like the arrow from the Tartar's bow it flies across the snows and over the seas until it rests its flight in the city by the sea! And even there it loiters not so fondly at the Rialto, or before St. Mark's, as beside the Adriatic, with the coasts of Dalmatia beyond, and still beyond the clouds, Greece and Athens.

THE STORY OF A MOTHER.

THE record of her early life may be passed over, for this story is the story of a mother. While comparatively young, she was left a widow with eight children. Her married life had been bright, her home happy. The conditions of life in those days were not easy; but her husband had been a man of courage, industry, and integrity, and with great faith and resoluteness they were laying the foundations of success, when death brought widowhood to her.

The struggle which followed, was that which has been with widowed ones since the world was: but with fine fortitude, energy, and patience, she kept her brood of children with her, and the home unbroken. She fortunately was endowed with qualities that fitted her for the struggle that lay before her. She was resolute, resourceful, broad-minded, tactful, with native shrewdness and strength of mind; practical, yet with large imagination and humor that enabled her to see the other and softer side of life's hard ways. While without imperiousness, she had large pride of character. Her children were educated in all the principles of manliness, were taught to hate falsehood, to love justice, to be upright, to be scrupulously careful in personal attire, not to minister to pride but to manly and womanly self-respect.

With all her courage and strength of character, she never was anything but womanly. The tender graces of her life never hardened into masculine coarseness, under the asperities of life. Her sympathies kept sweet, mind and heart remaining always visionful, open, responsive to beauty, faith, trust, and love. The strength of her personality held the admiration of her children to the last; and so winning was her motherliness that their love was not simply devotion but homage.

Thus far this story has been the familiar one of daily life, — faithful, motherly devotion, unwasting love and sacrifice, — and then what? Usually neglect and forgetfulness on the part of the children for whom motherhood gives its life. In every-day life this, perhaps, is the familiar sequel; and there is nothing more pitiful than the neglect and forgetfulness that come to the mother in return for the sweetest sacrifices the world witnesses. Life comes from her with pain and sorrow; it is preserved by her solicitudes. Her every breath is a prayer to God for her children. Make others great, make these my children good, is her constant invocation. And the children go out into the world and become absorbed in its ambitions; the path back to the old home is infrequently trodden; visits to the old home become few and hurried; the tendrils of affection are untwined and soon are clinging to new homes and fresh interests. Pitiful are the excuses that mothers ever are ready to give for the neglect of children! How they strive to cheat themselves with little sophistries into believing that the inclination to come to them is thwarted by unwilling duties, that neglect is not forgetfulness! And yet in the mother-heart is the great yearning for a little morsel of her children's love. If they would only come! If only they wished to come! There is no heart-hunger in the world so great as this unutterable longing of motherhood for the sympathy, remembrance, and love of children. The world has no sadder or profounder tragedy than the loneliness of mothers, living in the old home with the memories of their children, yearning for their presence, longing for their love, and yet forsaken and abandoned by those for whom they would gladly die.

It is not that humanity is cruel-hearted that it is so forgetful of its mothers; it is only that it fails to understand the divinity of a mother's love, until parentage reveals, sometimes too late, in a new generation, the mystery of it all.

The significance of the life of the mother whose story is being told, is that her motherhood received the devotion and homage that belonged to it. Nowhere was motherhood more royally honored. The personality was rare that could so win and keep the devotion of children. What it was, cannot be defined, but it held child-love with lover-like fascination. The children had large place and interest in the world: they had many friendships; they had homes and children; but there was never abdication of the mother's throne, and their allegiance was never less than absolute. Wives and husbands came, — they in turn became friends and lovers; children were born, — their parent's mother became their idol, too.

This mother's children went out to find their work in life. They found large place and wrought high service. But the impulse of it all, the love of humanity, the world-wide faith, the large sagacity, the industrial and business enterprise, the far-reaching vision, the love of harmony and beauty, the forceful energy to win success, came from the father and mother who gave them life. And the mother's love found an answering love. The children not alone called her name blessed, but they made her life blessed. Great wealth came to one of her sons, and he esteemed it a privilege to make provision for her, and did so with royal bountifulness.

When old age was coming to her, and the energy of life was running low, it was seen that unless something could bring back the zest of living, the mother's days were numbered; and the thought came, that if a home was made for her that she could call her own, where she could have her children come as they used to come in the little cottage of her earlier life, there would appear a purpose for her living and life might revive again. And so she was asked whether she would like to have a home that she could call her own, where her children could come as they used to come, and she caught the meaning and the gladness of it; in the planning and the dreaming of it, energy came back, and the life that was stranded, under love's sweet and rising tides floated on and off into long and happy years.

So Castle Rest was built on the island that she loved; and it was her home. There she could see the river flow, note the pageantry of beauty, hear the music of the rippling waters, the dancing leaves, and the sweeter music of her children's voices.

When the leaves faded and fell around her island home, there was her other home, not less beautiful, in the midst of the great city, with every want anticipated and every luxury at hand. No emphasis need be placed on the costliness of her surroundings, the exceeding beauty of her homes, the graceful architecture of Castle Rest, its amplitudes and beauties. She had rare discernment in the appreciation of natural beauty, art, and the comforts of a refined and cultivated life. But she was simple-hearted and unostentatious. There are other mothers who are housed in splendor, yet who are hungry-hearted for that which the architect cannot build nor the upholsterer supply. But the beauty of her homes and the almost royal luxuriousness of her

living were only the smallest part of the lifelong tribute. The luxury was the gift not of ostentation but of love. She was worthy of all that could be done for her, for was she not "mother"? Back of it all there was a personal devotion, a personal service, that was more precious than anything that wealth could buy. It was no perfunctory sense of duty that brought her children back to her with swift and constant steps. Were she sick, the wheels could not turn fast enough that brought her children to her side; and no cares of home were so urgent as to keep the sons and daughters absent if they could minister to her comfort or her joy. For all the years in all the children's homes the mother's birthday was the central day in the year's calendar. Wherever she was, there they came as the doves to the windows, and with music, art, and pleasant recallings of the early days of " mother's life " brought to her homage that a queen might have envied. For that hour the sons kept their brightest wit, and the gladness of the year centred on this festal time of a mother's rejoicing.

So her life went on into extreme old age. For eighty-four years it unfolded, before the translation into the other life that grows not old.

And then the end came; not that the years had brought sorrow, that the zest of life was gone, or that the love that ministered grew weary, but that she had lived her appointed years and it was her time to die.

She was not old, counting life by its higher values; memory, vision, sympathy, all the faculties of life seemed unwasted. Her love of beauty was as keen, her wit as bright, her appreciation of the love and devotion of her children as quick as it had ever been; and there was something, too, in the atmosphere of love and devotion in which she had lived, that kept the body from growing old, as the pure air of higher altitudes forbids decay; and the hair was not whitened, nor the face scarred with years, but as she lay for burial among the flowers, she seemed as she was twenty years before.

There usually is something tenderly pathetic and pitiful in the death of aged mothers. The long journey is over, and the heart-wish for love and sympathy has ceased. The children bring at last, with tardy remembrance, the flowers they should have brought in life. to braid them into funeral wreaths, while memory recalls its pleasant visions, and regret at a neglect, that was lack of thought and opportunity rather than forgetfulness, stirs the heart and unlocks the fountain of unavailing tears. But for this mother, death was not welcomed because life was sad. It had all been sweet and beautiful. The heart had been fed even more bountifully than the body had been housed. With every yearning for affection satisfied, every motherly sacrifice answered by children's devotion, the children would not tardily rise up and, above her unconscious dust, call her name blessed. They had walked with her through all the dusty ways of life, not only to make smooth the highways of her pilgrimage, but to make her paths fragrant with love and homage.

This is the story of this mother's life; told not because she was happy beyond the lot of mothers in the mere appointments of outward living, but because motherhood, in her, received the consecration and devotion that belong to its divinity. Universal motherhood is honored wherever children give to mothers the sympathy and love which is their reasonable service. The last chapter of the life was like all the rest. Among the flowers, not of pride, but of affection, she was borne to burial. Tender words were simply spoken of the home-making mother, a song of faith was sung, and over the fields white with blossoms, through the opening leaves of spring, in one of the palatial cars which had made her son's name famous, she was borne westward, with the great fragrant cross beside her, to the old home, where she had lived in her early motherhood.

There are not many villages so beautiful as the little town of Albion, with streets elm-arched, with pleasant homes, and the blue waters of the lake far off on the horizon's edge. Here in the cemetery fair and beautiful, with winding paths and verdant dales and hills, is the place of the abiding of her dust. By her children she was laid beside the husband from whose dying hands they had received their mother as a sacred trust, to love and care for till this hour. And here, the trust fulfilled, they laid her with tears and flowers, while love and memory of pleasant years gave glad assent to the preacher's word, "Who is there like a mother in all the earth?"

THE HEROES OF ONE SHOW.

IN the summer of '64, I was a student in college. The long vacation was coming on, my home was far away, and I was desirous of seeing something of the world. I had read Taylor's "Travels in Europe," and had fired my youthful imagination with the perilous wanderings of Livingstone; but I had no aspirations to be a tramp like the former, nor a missionary among savages of cannibal tendencies like the latter. A three months' tour, not too far away from home to be out of the way of occasional remittances, was about the measure of my desires; and some light occupation which should not compromise my sophomoric dignity, nor compel too close an intimacy with hard work, I thought would enable me to see something of the world, have a good time, and put into my pocket a moderate balance against the casualties of the coming year.

Greeley's "American Conflict" had recently been issued; the people were interested in the war, and the book was having a large sale through the Northern States. Gold was at an enormous premium;

and if I could sell some of these books in the provinces, and receive my pay in gold, I could transfer my profits into legal tenders, to my very great financial advantage.

The country itself greatly fascinated me. It was a sort of terra incognita. I could, on a small scale, have a foreign tour; the sale of an occasional book would hardly detract from my time or pleasure; and I should not be out of the reach of the succoring arm of an indulgent father, if the venture in any way miscarried. So to Her Majesty's Dominions, as a disseminator of ideas, I determined to go.

But I could not go alone. I looked the boys carefully over for a chum; sounded, with all the sagacity of a conspirator, the most desirable ones, concealing beneath vague hints and suggestions my momentous purpose, lest others should take the cue and become rivals in the profitable work of carrying the "American Conflict" across the border. At last I found a friend after my own heart, — a good-natured, easy-going, mild-tempered, ingenuous youth, full of mirth, "a fellow of infinite jest," the ideal chum for a wild-goose voyage. As the young man has since become a reputable college professor in the old Bay State, and has given every evidence of having outgrown the follies of his youth, I shall call his name Jones.

Our outfit was elaborate, based largely on prospective profits, — new satchels, resplendent with straps and clasps, new clothes, morocco note-books for reflections by the way, a brand-new canvassing book, with sample-backs pasted on the inside of the cover, an old trunk full of "Conflicts," a limited amount of cash, but high hopes; and we set our faces toward St. John, New Brunswick. Men of less enterprise would probably have gone to a second-class hotel; but we had not started out as second-class men, and nothing less than a front room in a leading house would satisfy our high ideas. Here I received, by previous arrangement, a remittance from home as a working capital.

We gave a few days to the quaint old city, lingered on its wharves, studied the curious fashion of its ships, and watched with never-failing delight the hurrying swirl of the tides, which came pouring in like great floods from the Bay of Fundy. The flavor of English life was delightful; the curious houses, the quaint signs, the dialect of the people, the methods of business, the numberless oddities that stared at us from all the alleys and by-ways of the town, made the hours pass unheeded, while the obsequious servants of the house received our orders with becoming humility, and our little store of sovereigns melted like wax in our prodigal fingers. Regularly after the pleasures of the day, its sentimentalisms were transcribed in bulky letters and sent across the line to the special young ladies who, long since having comfortably married other men, shall be nameless here forevermore.

A depleted treasury roused us from the delights of our provincial Capua. We sat down to plan the active work of the campaign. We took the map and traced the railroad lines. The names of the places were unattractive to our collegiate taste, refined by our intimacy with "the beauties of Ruskin," and the refinements of our budding "culture." At last we spied the name of "Sussex Vale." Here was the place. How visions of English scenery, the far-famed Sussex of Old England, came to us! And the word "vale"! Why, there was poetry and music in the very letters of the word! And both together, Sussex Vale, who could resist the combination? "Was it a large place?" We did not know! "Was it a wealthy place?" We did not ask! We had come down partially for pleasure, and there was no reason why "The Conflict" could not be sold as well amid beautiful as amid poor surroundings! And so to Sussex Vale, far up the road, we went.

A lean, long, lank, straggling town, with but few shops, an hotel, a few sporadic houses, and a mild flavor of musty decay formed the reality of the Vale, which had captured our youthful imagination.

We first visited a shoemaker's shop, told our plain, unvarnished tale, and solicited an order. We got it, but it was an order to get out. "Greeley was a Yankee blackguard, the Northerners were cheats and cowards, and the Southerners were brave; and the rebellion would wipe out the whole confounded Yankee nation, and the sooner the better." To be candid, our first reception left nothing to be desired in the way of warmth. We had expected, with the new suits and college culture and address that distinguished us, to cause some excitement, but we had not expected that the whole cobbling interest of the lower provinces would rise up at us, as it evidently seemed inclined to do.

We were ready, however, for either a scrimmage or sale. Was I not the crack oarsman in "The Undine," the college boat, and did I not know that it would be simply impossible to put Jones out, simply from his *vis inertiæ?* So in we sailed. The shoes were left uncobbled, while the "American Conflict" raged over discarded last and lapstone.

Never did those rebel craftsmen use leather better tanned, or threads better waxed, than we tanned and waxed them, for we were fresh from the debates of the old "Theta Delta" and "Zeta Psi" fraternities, and were as ferocious little patriots as ever for any purpose crossed the line of Her Majesty's Dominions. We were, moreover, in those intellectual horse-latitudes which intervene between a young man's freshman and sophomore years, — the period in every man's life when his mental powers reach the culmination of their growth, and when his conscious wisdom burns with a brilliancy never afterward possible of attainment.

We did not convert the cobblers, but they did not put us out, so we scored one for the stars and stripes, and went on our rejoicing way. At every house we found an enemy; at the post-office we got into a perfect nest of Southern sympathizers; but we stood our ground, and the harder the British Lion roared, the more we made the Eagle scream. The Vale did not impress us, and we had evidently failed to impress the Vale; so at nightfall we went on to an adjoining town, not selected on account of the euphony of its name. It had no hotel, but a stranger whom we met at the depot took us home, and gave us the hospitalities of his house — for a consideration.

The next day a most thorough canvass of that town was made. The men said "No!" peremptorily; and the women eyed us suspiciously, as they kept their feet against the door and thought of their silver spoons. Our money was getting low, and we had yet to sell our first book. So through village after village we took our weary way, the poetry of the trip gradually being rubbed off in our contact with the sturdy yeomanry of Her Majesty's Dominions.

At length we reached the little village of Hillsborough, on the Petticodiack River, — the town where the famous Albert Mines are located. Here we determined to make a stand and wait for reinforcements from home. I had previously written for remittances, but in the somewhat verbose answers that were returned not a word was said concerning funds. The weather was commented upon at aggravating length; family affairs were discussed; but there seemed to be a studied avoidance of the financial question. It was a big question with us, and getting bigger every day. At last I found it inconvenient to purchase the stamp necessary to send a letter home; and in a strange town, bankrupt, we poor, helpless, homeless tramps were hopelessly entangled in a web of financial troubles. Still we were happy. Introducing ourselves as young collegians out seeing the world, we played croquet with the fair New Brunswickers, flirted with them on the piazzas of their cottages and sauntered with them during the summer evenings on the banks of the unromantic Petticodiack. We sang our college songs on the veranda of our hotel, amid the gaping wonder of the gamins of the village; we were the heroes of village picnics, and were always booted and spurred for every expedition suggested by the young men, if after judicious inquiry we found there was no financial addendum to it.

The situation had in it some elements of solemnity. We had been at the hotel for many days. We were without visible or invisible means of support. Our entire assets consisted of a three-cent silver piece soldered so effectually onto a black iron watch-chain that I wore that it could not be made available for present needs. The old folks at home had evidently gone back on us. We were abandoned children,— too honest to steal, too respectable to beg, too well-dressed to work, too discouraged to peddle, too lazy to run away. There were moments when we calmly reviewed the situation and put to each other the unsolved conundrum, "What are we going to do?" But our sleep was sweet, our appetites never hung fire, and so long as our landlord was happy, we felt that we had no reason to be otherwise.

On one occasion we were on the verge of being scared. In the middle of the night I was awakened by Jones with the somewhat startling suggestion that he had the small-pox. I lit the lamp, and there sat bolt upright in bed the dumpy little tramp, broken out all over with what seemed to us the dreadful disease. We had not exactly calculated on this when we took the road. I gave all the comfort possible under the somewhat dubious circumstances; but the blotches flamed out red and ominous, and the three-cent piece on my iron chain looked mockingly at the two poor, abandoned, pest-stricken pedlers of republican ideas.

A somewhat solemn consultation with the motherly landlady of the house the next morning was followed by the welcome intelligence that it was an ordinary attack of the hives,—a harmless malady. There was not a guest at the house that ate his breakfast with a heartier relish that morning than Jones.

Well, at last the way opened out of our troubles. We were invited to visit the Temperance Lodge, our friends having found out that we were members of the order. We were called on to speak. Jones, fluent of speech, rattled off a good temperance talk. And I having, a few weeks before leaving College, been engaged to make a copy of a temperance lecture by one of the learned Pundits of the faculty, gave them about a third of the Professor's most admirable and elegant production, which, of course, was fresh in my mind. The thing took. It was not often that the dwellers on the banks of the sluggish Petticodiack heard such addresses, and they wondered and were silent. We then gave them some of our college songs, and our stock among the temperance folks was high.

On Saturday afternoon we addressed the Cadets, Jones telling some delightful stories, and I simplifying the second chapter of the Professor's admirable lecture. A comic song or two completed the conquest of the rising generation of Hillsborough. On Sunday the minister could hardly refrain from calling us out; on Monday night we were carried by the temperance people to an adjoining town, where Jones fired off some temperance common-places in his inimitably funny way, and I concluded the Professor's lecture.

Our fame was by this time widespread. It now began to serve us. In the printing-office of the place was a wild-eyed, long-haired, genial, good fellow, who aspired to the stage. Our performances had excited to undue activity his already inflamed ambition. Like all prophets he was not overburdened with the confidence of his native village; and he saw a chance, through our fame, to raise himself upon the pinnacle of renown. He waited on us and suggested that we get up a grand histrionic performance in the town-hall. He would join his talent to ours, and we could be sure of an overflowing and enthusiastic house. He was in the heavy tragedy line himself; and we could sing our glees and college songs, give a few readings and recitations of a lighter sort, and generally lighten up the somewhat sombre character of his heavier parts. At once light broke. We mildly suggested that we were not actors; that we scorned the base employment; that we were gentlemen, travelling through the country, hoping to add to our knowledge of men and things by our travels, etc., etc., yet if he thought, etc., why, we would be willing, etc. But in order to keep the hall from being monopolized by the small boys, would it not be better to charge a nominal fee, say of ten cents, etc., etc.? He thought it would, and so the contract was ratified then and there. He was to engage the hall, a piano, do all the printing, and we were to furnish with him the entertainment, and have the net proceeds.

His work was faithfully performed; and the barns and fences for miles around were covered with the flaring announcement —

"Messrs. —— and Jones, of the Mathetican Society, —— College, will give a Grand Literary and Musical Entertainment at the Town-Hall on such a night. At which time they will give Readings from Shakespeare, Recitations, Songs, Glees, etc., assisted by Hillsborough's well-known citizen, Mr. Blanck. Admission, ten cents."

The night came, and with it a rush. For a long hour before the show, the steady line of carriages and foot-passengers filed by the hotel, where we sat grinning and winking at each other as the priests in Cicero's time were said to do when at their sacrifices. We meandered up to the hall with becoming dignity, and the show commenced. Jones took the floor and addressed the house; stated that we had been invited by the culture and refinement of Hillsborough to give an entertainment; that we were merely amateurs, and craved the indulgence of the people. The thing opened with "Upidee," with tremendous emphasis upon the "roll" of the chorus, and tremendously accelerated speed on the last verses. It took, and the house was gained. Then came the local artist. His piece was "Bernardo Del Carpio." He came out with light chains upon his arms, knelt before his dead father, and with a clatter hardly excelled by the laughter of the prophet-stoning audience, he called down the maledictions of Heaven upon the treacherous king. We deemed it expedient to suppress the ambitious prodigy after his first effort, and unaided to carry on the rest of the show. We sang and read; we recited, declaimed, fired off college jokes and made ourselves as ridiculous as two impecunious tramps, struggling to get out of town, would be likely to do, under the stimulus of popular applause, far away from home. One of Jones' triumphs was the story of "Polyphemus." "Fuss at Fires" was one of my star pieces. The audience could never seem to get enough of the words "Don't forget to yell!" So when I, yielding to the impetuous encore, came out the second time, with that deference to popular clamor that marks the far-seeing actor, I interlarded the "Don't forget to yell!" with almost every sentence, — a thing the audience did not forget to do.

My crowning triumph, however, was the ballad of "Phebe Brown and Reuben Wright." The show was nearly over, the exchequer was full, we could leave town with flying colors, and I was laboring under a heavy pressure of success. The poetry of the piece was somewhat loose-jointed, and the story permitted infinite opportunity for changes and emendations; so I interjected local hits, such as came to me at the moment, and improvised verses that made up in appropriateness what they lacked in wit and rhythm. The old hall rang with the clapping of innumerable hands and thundered with the stamping of the heavy heels of the miners' boots; and flushed with success, unable to do the thing again, yet smiling sweetly and modestly, as though "such things were the habit of the man," I would only bow, and bow, and bow. They thought it was modesty, but I was stuck.

Jones gave the last piece, and should have dismissed the people; but I had tasted the sweets of popular success and wanted another chance. "That vaulting ambition that o'erleaps itself" impelled me to rush upon the platform. In tones of assured modesty I thanked the audience for their attention to the simple exercises of the evening, saying that if we had afforded them any pleasure we felt amply repaid, etc., and asking that we all rise and close by singing "God save the Queen." I knew that in Nova Scotia this was not an unusual custom, and supposed it was not here.

If there is one thing I am not up in, it is "God save the Queen." To this day I don't know whether it has one or twenty verses. I never knew even a single verse in anything more than the vaguest, merest outline. My ignorance of the piece was excelled only by Jones, who is to-day as ignorant of this loyal melody as he is of Sanskrit.

I relied on the audience, thinking it would carry

on the burden of the song. The pianist played it through. The audience rose, and I struck out, bold, strong, reliant, "God save our gracious Queen," but no one struck with me. Through the rest of the verse I was in the agonies of extemporaneous composition. Jones accompanied me loud and shrill, but without articulating a single word. Never did operatic singer mangle into a more unintelligible mass the words of her song than did Jones the unknown words of Her Majesty's melody; while with agony deep and prolonged, I evolved from my inner consciousness sentiments that I deemed appropriate for the somewhat solemn occasion.

Had we stopped here, my story would here end. The local artist who presided at the wheezy piano tripped off a little interlude and went on to the second verse. The very magnitude of the fix we were in, called forth all our resources. Without a smile we began to hum, and literally hummed the thing through from beginning to end. It had all the unity and completeness of a concerted tune, sounding much like a comb-band, without the twang of the loose teeth. It was the hit of the evening; the audience retired in ecstasies, and no man in all that region ever knew that we had not, with studied effort, saved the best wine for the last of the feast.

The door-keepers and our local friends followed us to our hotel with their congratulations. A neighboring restaurant which had not before thrived on our patronage answered with alacrity our liberal orders for cake, cream, and fruit. The friends went away, and the money-changers only were left.

The bills were paid liberally; every one who had contributed was generously reimbursed; and after it all, we found we had a sum of money left sufficient to pay all our bills and with a clear record to get out of town.

The next day, a responsible citizen waited on us, and offered a sum which seemed princely to us to go through the country with our exhibition. We shuddered, thanked him, and declined. We had many occasions, before we were back again in college, to regret our decision; and we have always had a lingering idea that when we declined to take the field as permanent minstrels, the one opportunity which always comes to every man once, and only once, was recklessly thrown away.

THE CONFESSIONS OF A BASHFUL MAN.

IF I had my life to live over again, and preliminary to my birth were offered a choice of gifts by the gods, instead of taking again the fatal gift of beauty I should surely choose the gift of confidence, — not that I would wish to be a confidence man, but using the term in the sense of assurance, or that other word which I cannot quite recall, which is the antithesis of bashfulness. Candor compels the confession that there is no family tradition of any star hovering over my nativity, as there was above Cæsar's cradle; but the good dames of the neighborhood, who assisted at the festivities of my inaugural, report that I lacked, even at my birth, the power of self-assertion; that I was suffused with blushes at the start, — the abashment of a modest and sensitive nature at the consciousness of its own nakedness, for I was a parson's child and was born poor, without a rag to my back.

In my early youth, with the exception perhaps of chilblains, my sufferings from bashfulness excelled the aggregated horrors of all my most cherished ailments, and I attribute most of my misfortunes to this impelling cause rather than to any wilful perversions or moral obliquities. The most optimistic of my friends — and in order to be friends they have to be optimistic — never gave me credit for having "the grace of a noble presence;" the actors do not come to hear me, as they came to Whitefield, to learn the postures of dramatic art. I attribute it all to the bashfulness of an untempered youth, which refused the lessons of the dancing-class, which might have made me a model of grace and elegance of bearing. The other fellows, who had courage which I lacked, always went home with the girls I coveted, and while they sauntered round by the longest way, left me to convoy home the wall-flowers by the short cuts. I was a bachelor until after twenty, because of bashfulness; and if I had been one of the cripples at Bethesda's pool, I should certainly have been one of the "leftovers" when the troubling of the waters ceased. The book that I shall write on the ministry, in the slippered pantaloon of my anticipated and pleasant dotage, will contain a chapter on the qualifications of the preacher; and while I shall say that honesty and piety, goodness, oratory, learning, and the summary of all the virtues are helpers to success, I shall also assert that confidence, monumental and complete, — underlying, overlying, interweaving, suffusing, overflowing confidence, — is the prime essential, without which all a parson's "life is bound in shallows and in miseries."

These are the general confessions of a bashful man. I will give specific instances of my humiliation. I attended once an Odd Fellows Picnic. It was during one of my earlier vacations, in one of the villages of Maine that is just on the outer fringes of the White Mountain region. I was young, and the people are always indulgent to youth. It was poor preaching that I gave them; but I was the best croquet-player in the town, and they pieced out the deficiencies of Sunday by the skill of Monday. I had been initiated into the order of Odd Fellows; and the scars of my ordeal were slowly disappearing when the lodge had a picnic on an island in the pond. I started out in life with a decided talent for picnics, but it was not encouraged. I was the parson's son, and shared in the utilities of the picnic rather than the pleasures, while the bent of my genius inclined to the frivolities rather than the materialities; that is to say, if there was a swing to carry, I was the committee on transportation; I climbed the trees, and hung the rope, and the other boys did the swinging. If the grove had to be raked up, the opportunity somehow came to me. It was felt that I had a basket-carrying talent which ought not to be neglected; and if my appetite for ice-cream is beyond that of my contemporaries, it is because while their youth was devoted to emptying the freezers, mine was spent in turning them. I had an accident once, too, at a picnic, which depressed me. It is not necessary to particularize, except to say that it was in the era of white pants and short jackets without skirts, and that it happened through jumping off a beam. It was not serious, but small accidents disconcert a bashful boy; and really, being pinned up with a handkerchief and having to give up the picnic, and back half the way home, was not a thing to enamour one of picnics.

Still, I went to the Odd Fellows Picnic because it was expected and the fees of my initiation had been remitted. They had a dinner, and were then to have some speaking. Nothing had been said to me about remarks; but I felt it in the lurid air of that summer day that I was to be the orator of the festival. It came to me that by omitting the closing dainties of the feast I could take a boat and row off on the pond, and inadvertently get detained until after the addresses; and so with a chance companion I started out. It was one of those quiet days when the surface of the water was like a polished mirror. The boat was hard, the sun was hot, the passenger was not the one at all that would have been taken if I had fled for companionship; but I rowed and rowed, turning deaf ear to all the blowing horns that called me back, haunting the remotest indentations, keeping behind concealing islands, fostering unrealizable anticipations in the spinster heart of my companion, all that I might keep away until the addresses might be concluded. I rowed around the pond until I could almost hear the frying of my brains in the tropic heat; and only when I made assurance doubly sure did I return, to hear, as my keel grated on the beach, the pleasant words, "You are back just in time. Your name has just been called!"

I have never had the consciousness of having unearned money in my pocket, — in fact, money earned or unearned has not greatly bothered either consciousness or pocket, — but I have for many years had a feeling that once at least in my checkered life I had received money for which I had given no adequate return. It happened in this way.

There was a town in Maine, where in the days of my early ministry I had many friends. I had dedicated the Masonic Hall with an address; I had preached the sermon at the dedication of the church; I had spoken at a picnic; and when the occasion came for the first celebration of the town on Decoration Day, who so fit to make the oration as the rising parson, who was settled on the sea-board fifty miles away? If I remember rightly, the father of the lady who was in the boat on the picnic day was the chairman of the committee, and it may have been that this was a factor in my selection; at any rate, I was asked to come and give the oration, and would be paid a goodly sum. It has been the misfortune of a life of many imprudences that the abnormal amiability which has been my bane always prompted me to promise services which were remote. If I were invited, by a friend whom I esteemed, to be hanged in thirty days' time, I should doubtless accept the invitation, although I should probably be sorry for it when the time matured.

I accepted the invitation, and spent the intervening time in getting ready for the effort of my life. Not to go too elaborately into the psychological secrets of bashfulness, it may be remarked, as this is a chapter of confessions, that a nature which is weak in confidence is strong in sentiment; and so I selected for my theme, "Heroism." The style was of the composite order, with a little of the efflorescence of the Byzantine period. The mythologies were enlisted, and the poets made tributary to the general effect; the classics added their color to the masterpiece; and Emerson and Carlyle, Ruskin and the later essayists, helped to make a rhetorical composition which would have delighted the heart of the teachers who correct the compositions in the ninth grade.

Well, the eventful day came. I was in the first barouche, which was designated in the programme as carrying "the orator of the day." The procession formed at the village square, and was something after this order as I remember it. The marshal, in cotton gloves (with other clothing, of course), the village band, un-uniformed veterans, barouche with "the orator of the day," accompanied by the selectmen, second barouche with resident ministers, — all sullen that the appropriation for oratory was not going to home talent, — other carriages containing citizens more or less distinguished, hay wagon trimmed with garlands, containing school children representing the "Nation's Hope," another band from a rival town, yeomanry in wagons, other yeomanry of inferior social grade on foot, small boys and cripples, — this was about the way of it. The marshal was about as ubiquitous as his horse, whose normal place was the hay-field rather than the field of war, would permit. The line of march was from the band-stand at the top of the hill to the graveyard; and the procession must have been as much as five minutes in passing a given point. In my younger days I was naturally of an observing turn; and before we reached the graveyard I began to think that perhaps "Heroism" was not exactly the subject best calculated to shake the hayseed out of the hearts of the auditory that I should have. The ride out was pleasant. None of us are unsusceptible to fame, and every one likes to ride in the first carriage in any procession, — unless it is a funeral procession; and I was not only human, but I was "the orator of the day," so catalogued in the programme.

By the time we reached the graveyard I was sorry that I was not to be left there. It would have been so sweet to die for one's country, or for anybody's country. Only to die and be at rest! Not to have to go back; to stop being "the orator of the day" then and there; to be a mute though inglorious Milton! Well, the soldiers spread their flowers, the children sang their songs, the marshal pulled up his white gloves and turned around his fiery untamed, and we moved, oh, how swiftly, to the place of my humiliation! If only to be an orator was to sit with the selectmen and look unconscious-like and self-possessed, as though one spent his time in barouches; to see fond mothers lift their children up to catch a sight, that they could tell of it to their children's children, — in short, to be "the orator of the day" is not so bad; but one must speak if he is to be an orator, and there's the rub. Well, we reached the town-hall, and I alighted. Followed by the clergy, as though I was going to my execution, I led the procession to the moderator's box. The band played; the children in arms wailed for the solitudes of the farm whence they came; and the chairman of the day introduced me with flattering remarks. It was no Ruskin-loving crowd that was before me; they had no hunger for finer shadings of rhetorical antithesis, and I knew it. Had I been other than a bashful man I should have let the classic figures rest, and have stood out before the people, and "made Rome howl;" unloosed the American Eagle, and set him flying over that bucolic multitude, told the story of the war, and made the welkin ring with patriotic platitudes. But, alas for speaker and hearer! I was a bashful man; and with a sense of humiliation which was like a nightmare, I spread out my double quire of perforated paper, and gave the mythologies of all the heathen gods. And the children cried, and I envied them that they could find solace in their tears; and the mothers trotted them, and cursed the madness that had made them seek the excitements of the giddy town; and the hired men shook the hayseed from their hair with their involuntary noddings; and the chairman looked wise as chairmen always do, and was bored as chairmen sometimes are; while the clergy were alert with puzzlings as to where the quotations were stolen from, having a kind of tiger-like defiance in their eyes that said to us, "We shall of course stand by you if there are any demonstrations." I have the oration yet. The blue ribbon is faded some; but I keep it, as the martyrs used to keep the scourges with which they had been beaten. I was not mobbed, but I should have been. The audience was somnolent rather than aggressive. I made it short, and hurried the heroes of the ages at a faster pace than Hood's pauper was hurried to his illustrious grave. There were no children held up to see "the orator of the day." The clergy congratulated me with their lips, while they whispered prayers that they might be forgiven for the falsehood; the chairman excused himself; the selectmen deserted me; the adulation of the earlier hours had spent itself; and the meanest of the heroes I had described was happier than I, because he was dead, and I was yet alive with the memory of my humiliation.

I had engagements in the village for several days, but I went from the town-house directly to the stable, ordered my horse, and in an hour's time was five miles away. I vowed that night that when the money came I would return it. But I was very busy and neglected to send it back; but not a hall or church have I dedicated since that day in that pleasant town, where I was once supreme, nor have I ever been asked again to come and serve them as "the orator of the day."

The opinion holds sometimes, in circles otherwise intelligent, that a minister is full of speeches, and is always on tap; that an introduction turns the faucet, and the speeches come by some mysterious law of loquacious gravitation. Every minister has his own little humiliations of this sort when he has been called upon for the "few remarks," the presentation of the prize medals, and the "surprise" to the teacher, who is not surprised.

I went to Greenwood once upon a Decoration Day, as a guest, I supposed, with no thought that I was to say a word; and only when, half an hour late, I reached the place, did I learn that I was booked to speak. It was not half a minute between the time of the discovery and the address. I hope that I acquitted myself with honor, but I am not sure. I can remember as well the substance of any other nightmare as I can recall the horrors of that speech; and it can be recalled now as well as it ever could be, for when the last sentence was finished and the reporter insinuatingly asked, "Will you give me the notes of your oration?" I indignantly and bewilderingly replied, "Why, man alive, I don't know a word that I have said!"

I was called upon once to present some bridal presents to a happy pair; and having no advisement of it, and being, as I have said, a bashful man, I began to hand over all the things that were in the region roundabout, and had with much elaboration presented the piano before I was told that the local furniture was not among the gifts.

I had in mind to say that the latest humiliation that had come to me as a bashful man was at a recent meeting of a Boston club. But then all the humiliations of my life are always new and never old. The first seems to be a thing of yesterday; and times and seasons bring no forgetfulness to these larger mortifications, which are the same yesterday, to-day, and forever. I had been invited not once but thrice to this association of worthies. I had prepared a paper years before and came on to Boston with it; but a friend who knew my weakness kindly died that I might be summoned home, and so the day of my humiliation was postponed. I had declined again and again with thanks, and pleaded work and refused, until it were ungracious longer to decline, and so at last I went.

The genial clerk who sent the invitations out, being optimistic in his temper, had promised an able paper. Of course he was not in my confidence, and did the thing to get the brethren there and collect the little arrearages that were hanging fire. I had an experience once in a Long Island town. I was to lecture for the benefit of the library. The subject of my lecture was something like the Art of Making Manhood, but the presiding officer had some mental twist, and introduced me with an elaborate description of my "Travels in the galleries of Europe, where I had studied the masterpieces of human art, which I would describe to the audience, from which he begged kind indulgence."

Well, if I went to Boston for a supper I did not get it; and if my plate was paid for, it was clean profit to the house. As an anti-appetizer, a speech, or even a paper before a Boston club, is a conspicuous success. In an elaborate study of this subject, it is proved to a demonstration that the big eaters are always put on to make the speeches in order to save the victuals. I have seen gormandizers of celebrity made as abstinent as monks in Lent simply by the intelligence that they would be expected to make a few remarks.

If old and hardened fellows are thus affected, what would be the natural effect upon a young and bashful man, who had been reared to think that Boston is the seat of culture, where every man is born a critic, and the pocket-knife in the pocket of every preacher is a lance to dissect the failings of weaker brothers? It would hardly be a fact to say that it was a night of revelry, or that Boston had gathered there her beauty and her chivalry. I might perhaps have represented the "shiveralry," but it would be hard to locate the beauty without invidious distinctions. But at any rate, if the American House had collapsed and become as the baseless fabric of a dream, some honored institutions of Boston and vicinity would have had hard sledding for a time.

One likes his friends generally, but not always. Imagination is a strong element in a bashful man; and while, on the night I am trying to describe, I was busy toying with the menu, I could invest the gentlemen around me with the associations of other days. Not ten feet from me was the honored ex-President, from whom in other days we used to get those "private admonitions," which were always deserved but seldom appreciated. In the midst of friendly chat I feared that he might remark to me that "after the reading of the paper he would like to see me in the President's office, to explain that little problem in physics, as to how the pumpkins were carried into the chapel, or the college cow precipitated into the neighboring reservoir."

It was whispered to me that I should be expected to have a "characteristic paper;" and when I asked what that meant, I was given to understand that it meant that I would "make it funny for the boys," though it was not put that way; and there before me, not forty feet away, was the Cambridge wit whose stories have wide currency. There was the Latin teacher not far off, who used to sit beside me in the class-room; and I could almost feel across the interval of twenty years the motion of an elbow, which meant a little help on that tough sentence in the ode of Horace, though it is not for me to say who owned the elbow and who owned the rib. There is the editor who knows good English; and three chairs away is the white-haired professor who has a scent for a mis-pronunciation like that of an Andover visitor for heresy; there is the professor of English literature, who is man enough, unless he has become corrupted by his associations, to stand up at the close of the coming trouble and say that "he had me for many years in charge and taught me all I know, and will the rioters in simple justice be kind enough to throw the missiles in his direction." And parsons! — why, they are as thick, in numbers I mean, as the leaves in Vallombrosa. Parsons to right of us, parsons to left of us! Editors, parish committees one of these days to be looking for "talent," a professor of modern languages directly opposite, so near that I can kick him for being here if I want to, — and I do, — and then just there at the left, where there is no escaping his basilisk gaze, is the old professor of mathematics. I used to like him, though I never told my love. He was the most genial and patient of men. Had he not been a saint, I should not be sitting here to-night; for I should have been the righteous victim of his wrath, and he would have been hung for murder. I had hardly seen him for twenty years, and the conscience which makes cowards of us all doubtless somewhat affected me; but I was in mortal terror through all the inquisition lest he might quietly remark, in those ominous blood-curdling words which have haunted me for all the years, "Mr. G., you may go to the board and put on the fourth problem." Well, these are only part of them; the room was full of them. It seemed as if —

> "The souls of all that I had murdered
> Came to my tent; and every one did threat
> To-morrow's vengeance on the head of Richard."

And so with that old, familiar, and fearful trepidation in the knees, I threw myself on the mercy of the court, hoping that it would be indulgent to a bashful man; and when I say that I was not mobbed, it will be apparent that it was.

THE SHADOW SIDE.

AS I look from my window at my neighbor's yard, I notice that while on the sunward side the snow has disappeared and the grass is green, beneath the windows that look northward the winter yet lingers. There are trailing vines and blooming plants in the windows on the sunny side, and children's faces are at the panes; and when the twilight comes there is a glow of firelight on the hearth and all the little tokens of a sweet home-life. But I have never seen children's faces at the panes upon the shadow side; indeed, there are double windows there against the winter winds.

If it is true, as the poet says, that

"In the grasses sweet voices talk,"

I wonder what will be the speech of the grass that yet lingers in its winter sleep beneath the belated snows. Will it not lament that luxuriant growth is denied it; and will it not grow sour with disappointment that its roots are anchored in the shadow rather than the sunshine?

Every life has its shadow side. Naaman was a mighty man in valor, but he was a leper. Saul was

Israel's king, but the people were singing David's praises beneath his palace windows. Haman was the king's favorite, but Mordecai refused to pay obeisance.

David was poet and king, but there was the spectre of his remembered crime. Solomon was rich with wisdom and the wealth of Ophir, but life was vanity of vanities. Peter was mighty among those who wrought wonders and subdued kingdoms, but in memory's chambers there were the echoes of the crowing of the cock. Among men none save Christ has wrought so largely in shaping the world's life as the Saul who was called Paul, but there was "the thorn in the flesh."

There is no joy comparable to that of literary creation. Out of the airy realm of the imagination to call forth invisible spirits, clothe them with living vestures, and make them unweave the tragedies and comedies of life; to give voice and speech to the dumb music that is in men's souls; to follow the elusive trails in which thought runs; to braid together the threads of fact and fancy; to weave words into literature, — there is in all the world no joy that equals the ecstasy of the mind's creative work. But, "except the Newgate Calendar," says Carlyle, "the biography of authors is the most sickening chapter in the history of man."

Milton writes the "Defence of Liberty," but his sightless eyes shall not see the laurels of his fame.

Goldsmith, Coleridge, De Quincey, Scott, Lamb, Leigh Hunt, Poe, Dickens, Carlyle, — every one has life's shadow side. Seven cities shall contend for Homer dead, not one for Homer living; and though Florence shall make merchandise of Dante's fame, there is no sadder sight in all the tragedies of literature than the exiled Dante going upon the hills and turning his hungering eyes toward Florence, which he could not enter.

The light fell with soft entrancement on Newstead Abbey, which was the poet's home; what other gifts could the gods give to this one, who had music for every song and an art to mirror Nature in all her moods? But there was the club-foot!

Hawthorne shall write the finest romance in American literature, but the pendulum of high ecstasies swings into mental depressions which are as night's thick blackness. When the grass grows long on the graves of the prophets, men gather the stones which crushed them and build them into the monuments of their enduring fame: but the only monument the prophets saw was the martyr's stake, and they died feeling that they were only

"The idle singers of an empty day."

So on life's lower levels every home has its shadow side; and every life has somewhere, in the seasons of its unfolding, "the winter of its discontent." "I cannot say," said the pastor of wide experience, "whether among the rich or poor I have found most unhappiness." There are heartaches as heavy in boudoirs as under the rafters of hovels; and within closets carved with rich traceries of art there are skeletons that lay burdens on hearts that beat with heaviness beneath costliest fabrics. "Every heart knoweth its own bitterness, and no stranger intermeddleth with its joy."

But every life has also its sunny side. Some one has said that life has two handles, — a bright one and a dark one, — and it is for us to say by which we will take hold of it. I used to go to see a poor misshapen, crippled boy. He was seldom free from pain; but out of his multiplied infirmities he had distilled a sweetness of spirit that made his cripple's chair a place of beauty, and his prison-chamber a place of brightness. He was never morose, never down-hearted, never felt that his life had a shadow side, because the brightness of his large faith and sweet content made even the darkness light about him. I was in one day to see him; and after his paroxysm of pain was over, and his face had taken on again its familiar smile, I said to him, "Well, you do have a hard time of it!" and with a look of wondering surprise he said, "Why, no; this is nothing to what it would be if I was blind!" There was just that little patch of sunshine in his life, — the fact that he was not blind; and in that he stayed, and refused to go around on life's other side where the shadows were. And in my searchings round the world I never found one who has so well found the philosophy of life as that crippled boy.

It was a hard stint we had before us, — to ride for two long days over the crest of the Rocky Mountains, on the bags and baggage that were on the top of the old stage. There were a good round dozen of us, and we had all been bred to gentle usage.

But there was no alternative ; and we could increase inevitable discomfort with our laments, or we could make our journey with mirth and laughter and such imaginings as would change it into a delight. And so we mounted to our place of torture with such smiles as we could summon : and we took our bruises not with grumbling or with a stoic's silence, but with laughter, as though each scar was a badge of honor, and every laceration was a caress. It took much imagination and great stores of philosophy ; but we loaned our laughs for one another's needs, and kept good-hearted, and so made the journey, which else had been a torture, with such sweet endurance and pleasant comfortings that now, when the bruises all are healed, we find in memory a sweet residuum of pleasant recollections.

The Hindoos tell the story of the man who had such rare art of divination that he could always see the soul of good in things evil. One day, to test him, they stopped with him beside the dead body of a dog, and his friend with disgust and bitterness spoke of it; but the wise man said, "But oh, how white his teeth are!"

If I remember rightly it was Southey who tells us of the woman that he met in one of his walks, who was so optimistic in her views of life that she had unquestioning faith that "whatever is, is right." He made to her the rather obvious remark that it was dreadful weather; to which she answered that "in her opinion any weather was better than none."

Sydney Smith somewhere says that the secret of happiness consists in taking short views of things. We are cursed by our imaginations. The iron of the dentist's forceps is not half so hard as our anticipations made it, although no one would assert that its caressings are as pleasant as the arms of the houris of Mahomet's heaven. The water of the river in which we used to swim always was colder when we shivered on its banks than when we swam in its currents; and the physicians say that the pain of dying is not half so great as the dread of it.

After all, our estimates of life are relative. "A one-eyed man is king among the blind;" and it is well for us, in choosing our standards, to look down and not up. We envy the richer man, whose liveried footmen sneer at us. Do we not know that, though we drive our own modest equipage, the man who owns the mule envies us our horse; and the man who walks envies the man his mule; and the lame man envies the man who can walk; and the man who is without legs would be content to be lame if only he had legs at all?

There is a story somewhere of the wise man in abject want, who was eating some garden stuff which he had picked up; and he said to himself, "Surely there is no one in the world more poor and wretched than I am;" and he turned and beheld another man eating the leaves which he had thrown away.

I was sick and weary-hearted with over-burden of my cares, and I went and sat in the home of an aged woman whom I had known long and well, and with querulous complainings I was bewailing my weariness; and as I talked I looked upon the wall before me, and there I saw the pictures of six stalwart sons to manhood grown, every one of whom had gone away from this mother's home to sail upon the sea, and one by one had been lost upon the deep. And in the face of the larger sorrows of this sunny-hearted woman, who was thanking God by day and night for the faithful daughter that remained, how small and petty, yea, how wicked, seemed my little sorrows!

Oh, but this staying on the sunny side of the house, instead of living on the shadow side of life, is the very art and philosophy of living. How much does the art of seeing the sunny side of things do to make life go smoothly! There are Aunty Dolefuls whose coming into the home so darkens life that we have to raise the curtains to see our work. There are physicians whose countenances increase the temperature and quicken the pulse. We do not wonder that Charles Lamb loved Jem White and lamented when he died because half the gayety and sunshine of the world had gone.

Sunniness of temper is the mark of a gentleman; and it was a wise test of a gentleman which Thackeray puts into the mouth of one of his waiters when he makes him say, "Oh, I knew he was a gentleman, he was so easily pleased." Life is not all shadow nor is it all sunshine, but it has its sunny and its shadow side; and often it is for us to say whether we will live on the sunny side, where the grass grows green and the flowers bloom, or on the shadow side, where the winter lingers yet with its snows and frosts. Often where the shadows are we can bring such inward sunshine of the spirit that even the shadows may flee away. And this resource is left to us, — to endure the burdens with a courage that shall make them light. Paul prayed God to take away the thorn; and God refused because he wished to do a better thing for Paul, and so He gave him strength to bear the pain.

What a beautiful story is that of the gentleman

who, visiting the deaf and dumb asylum, wrote this question on the board, " Why did God make you deaf and dumb, and made me to speak? " The eyes of the little ones filled with tears; it was a great mystery; their cleverness knew no answer. Their faith solved it. One went to the board and wrote, " Even so, Father, for so it seemeth good in thy sight." So if there is no way out of the shadow side of life, if the burden will not drop, there is left for us the sweet assurance that " My grace is sufficient for you;" and so because the shadow seemeth good for us by Him who in love has appointed the ways of life, we may know that somewhere in the heart of the sorrow there is the hiding of a blessing which will at some time be revealed.

WITH THE RANK OF CAPTAIN.

WE never knew just how it happened; but there the commission was, signed and sealed, making us Chaplain of the corps, "with the rank of Captain." If we had the rank, we surely had the title; and so we were to be called Captain! We had never dreamed it!

Our antecedents were ecclesiastical rather than military. There was a rumor that on the maternal side we had come in direct descent from Elder Brewster. But the elder was a preacher, not a soldier. There were traditions, too, of a certain ancestor on the Cape, who had held important military rank in the good old colony days; but the annals were not clear, and the impression held that the ancestors had wrought their deeds in other fields than those of war. Still, it ought to be said that our genius is not of the genealogical order. We have always maintained that when one has traced the family back far enough to get a fairly good ancestor, it is wise to stop. He may go farther, and fare worse. There was nothing in our own youth to indicate a military career. Of course, no one can tell what his biographer may find; but our own remembrance gives no stronger hint of military leanings than the fact that on one disastrous June training-day, in our early adolescence, we peddled lozenges on the muster-field, — the incident being impressed on us from the fact that the sales were as poor as were the confections which we were subsequently obliged to eat. We had, of course, paraded in the Cadets of Temperance; but that was a social company with a reform attachment, and was neither militant nor triumphant.

We had served briefly in the War of the Rebellion. The service was brief, — but three weeks in length. It was not hard, as the hotel where we boarded had a good table, and we went home nights. We could not get the parental signature to the enlistment blanks, and so were mustered out before we were mustered in. That is the reason why until the present we have been without a military record. And now, by this blessed commission, we were appointed "Chaplain, with the rank of Captain." No working up from low subalternism, but jumped as it were from private station to a post of honor, — a kind of second Cincinnatus business of going from the plough to the throne, although of course we never had a plough and have no throne, although we hold the Captain's rank.

It may be necessary to remark to those who are not connected with the regular army or the State militia that a military commission is not only the designation to an office, but is a command to the officer's subordinates to obedience; and so following the appointment "with the rank of Captain," appeared the words, "and he is to be respected and obeyed as such."

We have never had the lust of power; but, to put it mildly, we were pleased at the new title that had come. To be called Captain, instead of parson, dominie, elder, and doctor, was a relief if not a promotion. To be respected as a captain was delightful; to be obeyed as a captain was blissful. The only thing lacking which the colonel omitted in sending the commission was a military guard to execute the order. We read the document with every variety of inflection and intonation; but even in our own family, where we were measurably obeyed as a husband, we were derided as a captain. We told the colonel of it; he sadly smiled, and said that the same condition existed in his own home. It was one of the effects of a lack of military background.

Well, the first campaign came. The march was not hard from the armory to the depot where the corps embarked. Of course, a soldier's first march is always trying; but the springs of the cab in which we rode were easy, and the driver went by the smoothest streets. Philadelphia was reached in good form; the mayor received us, and we were dismissed for parade at two o'clock. While we are waiting for the fateful hour, it may be said that the corps on whose staff we were an officer more or less distinguished, "with the rank of Captain," is not included in the State or National Guard, but is one of those pleasant social companies like the Old Guard, the Ancient and Honorable Artillery, the Putnam Phalanx, and kindred organizations. The members are gentlemen; their campaigns are bloodless; there are many banquets but no battles; delightful companionships are created; and incidentally the military spirit is fostered by the picturesque continental uniform, the striking military marches, and the martial music. Nearly all the great cities which the company has visited have welcomed it with enthusiasm, and the annual field-days and excursions have been memorable.

At two o'clock we were in line, the "Chaplain, with the rank of Captain," among the staff. We had never been in uniform before; before the day was over, we vowed internally and externally that we would never be in it again. And yet the uniform was very striking and becoming.

A swallow-tailed-coat, with bright brass buttons; a vest with buttons also bright; cocked hat and plume; white kid or cotton gloves surmounted with the jauntiest lace; with touches of buff, and straps and fixings, velvet breeches, and boots immaculate with yellow tops.

Altogether the uniform in military circles would be called "striking," in female parlance "lovely," in the realm of dudedom "swell." Every man in the ranks knew this, and this was why the wives were happy to have their husbands join the corps. The Chaplain's uniform was not quite so fascinating as that of the other men: but while the sombre proprieties were observed, it recognized the fact that preachers are human, and the names of their wives are Vanity. The hat was not tipped with quite so rakish a pitch; the buff decorations were used sparingly; the top-boots gave way to shoes; the frills and ruffles were less abundant, though judiciously administered they could be made quite effective.

We confess that when we stood for the first time in our place, in the corridors of the hotel, preliminary to marching orders, we were abashed by the gravity of our honors and the ridiculousness of our clothes. We could stand the swallow-tail, and were oblivious of the cocked hat because we could not see it. But the knee-breeches and the stockings were the source of our humiliation. We had hitherto been fully dressed, and the sight of our own unsheltered, undisguised extremities abashed us. We simply were not used to it; we were, so to speak, the slave of the conventional, and we missed, oh, how we missed our customary costume on the long, long march through the streets of the Quaker City!

The march began. We had never kept step with mortal man before. We got the wrong foot first, and half the time were hitching up a lost step, like an interfering horse. The gamins followed along the sidewalks, and the factory girls applauded from the windows; the other members of the staff marched like veterans, while the Chaplain, outwardly assuming a hero's mien, inwardly wished he had worn his other shoes and had on his longer pants. But the band of forty pieces played the tunes the Chaplain liked; and if there had not been the spectres beneath of the ribbed stockings moving in and out, his heart would have been happy. Well, the longest march even in knee-breeches must end at last; and in the armory of the State Fencibles, who were the hosts, the corps was entertained with lavish hospitality.

The striking uniform of the company is easily carried when many are together, but when one wearing it is alone, he is usually taken as an escaping freak from some dime museum. With this uniform on, there is only safety in numbers. We did not know it then. We are now sure of it.

Well, the boys were tarrying at the banquet. We felt homesick for our normal clothes and sighed for our satchel. It was fairly dark as we started for the hotel a dozen blocks away.

The blocks in Philadelphia are miles in length, and the city evidently has the best electric lights upon the continent. Why, every vest-button seemed like a calcium light, and the brasses on the swallow-tail were like the headlights of a locomotive. The streets had no shadow side, and the whole town was out that night.

Dante has described a trip through purgatory, and the particulars of that evening's journey can be omitted. We will give but one incident as a kind of sample brick. We were getting along fairly well, trying to keep the ribbed stockings as much in the shadow as the shop-windows and the electric lights would permit. A wicked, wizened little Quaker, who ought to have been at home like an honest man, trotted up beside us, and looked at us while he trotted. Pretty soon he said, in a little drab-colored piping voice, "My friend, that is a very beautiful and picturesque costume you have on, but I hardly think you will be able to get the world to put it on again." This was the last humiliation. We could stand the jeers of the gamins and the admiration of the factory girls, the sarcastic interrogations of the irreverent as to the name of the museum where we "held out;" but to be taken for a dress reformer, a kind of masculine Mrs. Bloomer, was to fill the cup to the overflow, and make us regret that we had ever accepted the rank of Captain.

We could go no farther. The ribbed stockings refused to move. The Captain turned and looked at the shrivelled-up remnant of expiring Quakerdom, and as he held him by the button, said in a voice meant to be admonitory, "My friend, if you are as much of a Quaker as you seem to be, and the Quakers are as kind as they are said to be, you will keep still about my clothes. I know they look pretty bad, but they ain't a circumstance to the way I feel."

The Quaker disappeared, and we jogged on more in sorrow than in anger. But somehow the solitary march that night disenchanted us of our dreams of military glory, and took away much of the pride we had when we were commissioned "Chaplain, with the rank of Captain."

THE STUDENT'S WORKSHOP.

IT is not easy to dissociate historic from intrinsic beauty, and to tell to which it is that a place owes its magic charm. A simple field ripens its harvests all unnoticed until a poet crosses it and drops beside its paths the broken garlands of his song, and ever after it is a place of pilgrimage; the singer carols his song beside "ye banks and braes o' Bonny Doon," and henceforth the grass-grown walks become worn with footsteps; in the quaint churchyard at Stoke Pogis, Gray writes his immortal elegy, and those who pass unvisited the proud castle on the hill beyond have time to linger here beneath the yew-tree's shade and talk of that to which all greatness comes, as they muse among the graves. At Oxford, Addison's Walk is visited, though the famous races in the outskirts are unseen; while the study of the Wizard of the North at Abbotsford arrests the steps of those whom Holyrood is powerless to hold.

The magic hand of Longfellow touched the little Minnesota Falls and changed them into the "Laughing Waters;" the poets have found the old legends of Yosemite, so that now the gentle Merced sings its old-time ballads to El Capitan, and hallows the valley with the presence of invisible spirits; the Yellowstone Park excels Yosemite in grandeur of wonders, but no poet has woven over its brilliant canyons the gossamer of his legendary songs, and the great world not yet has turned to its holy shrines the feet of worshippers. Disraeli and the many others who have written of the life and history of authors have said but little of the places where men have written the great masterpieces of literature. Scott's study remains as it was when he laid down the sovereign pen; but how little we know of the places which men would make into shrines if only they knew where they were. From the works of many of the great writers the outlook from the windows can be learned, because the outward surroundings insensibly register themselves upon one's thought. We know that Tennyson looked upon the sea while he wrote, for the beating waves have left their music in the rhythm of his verse; sunny Nature touched the novelist's study table at Gad's Hill, for its shining suns have gilded the beauty of his creations; the moorland spread beneath the windows of the Brontë sisters, for everywhere there is heard the plaintive wail of the desolation that broods above the marshes; while we shall find that the trees of Rydal Mount have dropped their leaves upon Wordsworth's songs. The

Grub Street attics have photographed their poverty in the writings of their occupants; and as De Quincey's early hunger shaped the moods of his later life, so the physical environments of the student, artist, or author give color and flavor to their created works.

It is curious, too, that in the writings of men there are so few allusions to the places where they have wrought. Poets have written of the brooks by which they paused, the woods in which they wandered, and have not been slow to pay tribute to the outward surroundings that have ministered to them. Still, how few of them have drawn for us the picture of the rooms in which they did their work! The landscape has left its features in their songs; but seldom have they told of the shelves upon the walls, the dusty folios, the familiar table, the writer's chair, the narrow spaces, in which, with "gentle pacings," the immortal work has been evolved. Leigh Hunt saw Lamb in his study take down and kiss the old folio; yet this genial writer, who has said the sweetest things in literature of books and their places, has told us little of the spot where he created the sunniest essays ever written, and only by imagination can we see the room where he found the joy of living, and where on some day he hoped to lay his over-beating temples on a book and have the death he envied.

His study must have been a tiny place, for he used to say that he liked contact with his books. He loved to touch them, to have a table high piled with books behind him, a writing-desk beside a warm fire at his feet, having them all close by, so that if the wind came in he could fence it off by his precious books. The Archbishop of Toledo wrote his homilies in a room ninety feet long. The Marquis Marialoa must have been approached by Gil Blas through whole ranks of glittering authors, standing at due distance. Montaigne had in his great château a study, "sixteen paces in diameter, with three noble and free prospects." Epictetus preferred a little spot, large enough only for a stool and chair; while Milton believed in the hospitality of knowledge, and wrote:

> "And let my lamp at midnight hour
> Be seen in some high lonely tower."

The genuine student's ideal study is of double character. There is the library with its long rows of masters, the rare editions in every department of art and knowledge, — the choice Aldines, Bodonis, Elzevirs; and beyond this is the working "den," — a closet-like room with rude chair and table only, with nothing on the narrow walls, windowless, save for the light that comes from the panes set high in wall or roof. Here, with no distraction, the mind and pen can work together, the silent counsellors in serried ranks in the room beyond, guarding against intrusion and sending in the invisible influence of their mighty yet speechless presence. The rain beats noisily upon the roof and walls of the little den; the floor is littered deep, for no profane eye sees this inner sanctuary; it is a place of dreams, a mount of visions, entered only when the mind is girded for its work and would fight its battles in solitude. In the midst of the White Mountains there is a place like this, where a working author to whom the summer brought only partial rest performed his daily task. It was in the attic of a summer hotel, in an unplastered room; a rude box was his chair, a board his table; no curtain was at the window, no carpet upon the floor, nothing of comfort or ease. But here by the open window the gifted one would sit enraptured by his thought, and the purple clouds would shed their glory on his page, and the story of the laughing skies, the annals of the eternal hills, would come and bid him be their interpreter to a waiting world.

On the New England coast there is the study of a genial writer of tales. From the driftwood of the shore he has fashioned a little hut just above the waves. The broken spars that form the walls are rudely covered with boards between which is the fibrous turf matted thick with wild sea-grasses; the roof is covered with refuse tin which the roofers of the village have discarded; and beside the walls, with clumsy masonry, a chimney has been built like the wide-rooted ones that the Normans used to make. The house is tiny in its inner proportions, with a floor of native earth trodden hard into such uneven surface as is beneath the fair mosaics of St. Mark's at Venice. There is a rude table of unpainted wood, and by it a chair platted with crude handicraft of native rushes; and beside the sooty fireplace is a rocker of such enticing curvature of back as makes it the fit place for dreaming dreams beside the fire.

In a New England town there is a study that realizes one's ideal of the environments of a contented literary life. Outside a thriving town, hardly ten minutes walk from the centre of its little life, a pleasant home lies half hidden behind its hedges. It has green blinds after the New England fashion, and sits in the midst of a great yard walled round with currant and other bushes. There is everywhere an atmosphere of comfort, for the great farms are just beyond, with hospitable sheds, painted red without, and clean with newest whitewash within. The grass is green with the peculiar lustrous hue of English turf, always short, as though the cattle were allowed at times to feed upon it and sweeten it with their breath. In the midst of the yard a miniature house is set, white-walled, green-blinded, just beyond the outmost spread of the maples, where it can catch all the light and sunniness. This is the study of the proprietor of this home with its rich acres beyond. The books gathered in a life of semi-leisure are upon the shelves;

the open fireplace is in the walls; rugs made from the skins of beasts shot in earlier days are upon the floor; and all the trophies of the years — the oars and foils of college days, the fishing-rods of the days of sport — are gathered here in this pleasant place. From the windows every part of the estate can be seen; and at the door, just where, from the old step, the saddle can be mounted, is the hitching-post, where the convenient horse stands waiting to bear the owner to the supervision of the fields, and then back again to the accustomed chair. This, to the average student, would be the ideal life, town and country touching each, — a life of study mingling with one of easy yet successful manual toil.

There are not a few studies created by great wealth. In Germantown, just outside of Philadelphia, a well-known banker has erected probably one of the finest libraries in the United States. The building adjoins his house, which is one of the princely dwellings of the city and furnished with all the elegance that cultivated taste and unlimited wealth can devise. The library is lighted mostly from the roof, though there is one large window opening toward the finest view upon the estate. The walls are tinted with neutral colors, though on the ceiling there are chaste decorations such as befit a place of books. Carved oaken cases extend around the walls, and on them are all the great masters of the realm of literature. Wealth has imposed no limits upon desire; and here are the masterpieces of the ages, set in such royal bindings as bewilder and delight. Upon shelves and brackets, walls and mantels, there are a student's costly instruments, a telescope for the infinitely great, microscopes for the infinitely small, globes, charts, maps, costly vases disinterred from buried cities, ornaments of Etruscan art, trophies rescued from Homeric lands. The poor student, who has been wont to exult in his costly treasures, returns home with a sense of infidelity, because in the presence of fairer treasures he has been momentarily unfaithful; and never again is there quite the old pride in the presence of the little hoards which have so sorely taxed his scanty purse.

There are two things at least that are essential in the equipment of the well-furnished study. The first is the open fire. The study must of necessity be free from all human occupants save its owner, and yet there is need of some sense of life. Scott found it in his dogs; others have had their pets of various kinds. The open fire seems to give the subtile companionship that is needed. Whether it is because there is motion, transformation, an apparent process of life, I am not philosopher enough to say; but fire has always been among men a deity of worship, and in the lowest and highest civilization has been regarded not simply as an instrument of service, but as having a sort of sympathy with men. There is nothing in the range of lighter essayists more quaintly human than the fireside reveries of Marvel. There is little of virile philosophy in these imaginings, and one does not well to take these reveries when he would gird himself for life's great work. But for its meditative hours, when the spirit loves to deal in retrospections, there is no friend who can with subtler sympathy enter into the mood of the spirit, and bring back the pleasant visions of forgotten days better, than the fire within the grate.

In addition to the library fire there ought to be somewhere in the dustiest corner a solemn, large-eyed owl, — the only creature ever made by Mother Nature as the embodiment of wisdom, and therefore fitted to be the literary deity of the student's study.

There are dark horses in literature as in politics, and there are those who have the gift of silence. This is the owl's strong point. He is not loquacious; he is as silent as the tombs of the Capulets. His plumage does not excite envy; his flesh has the reputation of being as tough as a publisher's conscience; but he looks as wise as a mathematical professor. In the British Museum there is a large case of owls; and one may travel from the Blarney Stone to the Hanlin Yuan of China without finding such an assemblage of wisdom as glares from the glass eyes of these feathered philosophers.

Beyond, however, all outward furnishing, to the

genuine student every place is ideal in its beauty where rest his beloved books. Hawthorne could transform into a palace an old country inn with no other wand than an old directory; while Lord Strangford made his hour's delay at the railway station a delight by tracing out the etymology of the names in Bradshaw's Guide. Housed in hovels or in palaces, the student's library is his place of joy, and once among his beloved books, he can say with Machiavelli: " I pass into the antique courts of ancient men, where, welcomed lovingly by them, I feed upon the food which is my own, and for which I was born. Here I can speak with them without show, and can ask them the motives of their actions, and they respond to me by virtue of their humanity. For hours together the miseries of life no longer annoy me; I forget every vexation : I do not fear poverty ; and death itself doth not dismay me, for I have altogether transferred myself to those with whom I hold converse."

THE PARSON'S SMALL BOY.

THERE is a German proverb which declares that one can never be too careful in the choice of his parents; and if I had my life to live over again, I should at least hesitate before allowing myself to be born into the world as a minister's son.

To begin with, he is born with a bad name, the old saying about ministers' sons and deacons' daughters creating an atmosphere of suspicion around the cradle in which rocks the male heir of a parson's family. From observation of the world, I am satisfied that the old saying has suffered in translation, and that the original manuscript gives the bad name to the ministers' daughters and the deacons' sons, — a conclusion that has received the commendation of not a few of the masculine scions of the clergy.

Then this being born as a kind of ecclesiastical baby is not pleasant. There is an excess of attention from which a timid child naturally shrinks; while the sense of proprietorship on the part of all the parish matrons, bringing the consciousness of being a sort of church baby, is confusing to the infantile mind.

Other babies are permitted to enjoy the usual childish ailments in comparative peace; but every amateur nurse in the parish feels free to try her nostrums on the public baby. I shall not permit myself to be ungracious to the super-serviceable old ladies who lent a hand in the measles crisis, nor add an extra pang to the avenging consciences of the old maids who added new horrors to the chicken-pox catastrophe. I can feel the tightening of their bandages even now, and, to my mind at least, the fabulous depravity of a parson's boy is simply a feeble attempt to pay back to the world some of the sorrows it has caused him to suffer in earlier years.

Reasoning, however, from the old axiom that the most amiable persons are evolved from the crossest babies, I am reasonably assured that the lives of my earlier tormentors did not consist of bliss wholly unalloyed, — a fact that has received the verbal confirmation of the guardians of my youth.

I shall pass over in forgiving silence the catalogue of the sufferings inflicted by my multitudinous nurses, having, I trust, a more forgiving though not less observant mind than the poet who wrote the following lines: —

> "I recollect a nurse called Ann,
> Who carried me about the grass,
> And one fine day a fine young man
> Came up and kissed the pretty lass.
> She did not make the least objection.

> Thinks I, ' Aha!
> When I can talk I 'll tell mamma.'
> And that's my earliest recollection."

Emerging from the cradle-stage, I passed into the errand-running period, inevitably present in the career of a minister's son. My legs were in perpetual motion in the church's interest. If a levee was in progress, who so naturally as the minister's son should run for the key of hall or vestry, build the fires, and carry the notices? If the church was to be decorated at Christmas, the parson's boy must pull the evergreens; at the "Old Folks' Concert," he must carry the dishes and borrow the settees; and if I should outlive Methuselah, I could never eat half as much ice-cream as at church festivals I have frozen, though it is said that I am not without some talent with the spoon and saucer. Then the chorister must be supplied with weekly hymns, the sexton notified, sewing-circles generally waited on; and while I never resented the preparations for the fairs, I used to bewail the lonesomeness of sweeping up the hall and carrying home the properties after the festivities.

The minister of thirty years ago in the Massachusetts towns was generally on the school committee; and for the sake of lightening the labors of our teachers, they were told that if we had need of punishment we should be sent home, where the ceremony would be performed with thoroughness and despatch. We could never quite see why, when the teacher was paid for this sort of thing, the minister's sons should be neglected, though perhaps our own æsthetic sense, which preferred a light rod in the school-room to a heavy one in the domestic woodshed, had something to do with our discontent. It was very annoying to a youth intent on learning to have his studies broken in upon by being sent home with notes asking the favor that the bearer be flogged and returned; and if there are occasional gaps in my knowledge of the occult sciences taught in my boyhood, it is perhaps owing to the above-mentioned absences, which it is due to myself to say were not of my own seeking. I knew, however, that this arrangement was largely an official one, intended for effect on the other boys, and therefore seldom went back for a duplicate, if in the transit from the schoolhouse to the woodshed the original note was lost.

A quarter of a century ago was the golden age in New England of denominational associations. At such times, the minister's small boy became general martyr to the church at large. By day, he was the pilot of the delegates to their houses of entertainment, and the burden-bearer of the noon collation; while at night, after his own bed was monopolized by the brethren, he could take his choice of such portions of the floor as were not occupied by other members of the family.

As I remember the days of my youth, our church had an itinerant ministry, and our house must have been on the general line of travel. Mr. Beecher complained that his church was nothing but a spiritual hotel; our house in the old days was a clerical tavern, and never without a good business. I was as glad to see the brethren as the hospitable parents; but to say that I enjoyed doing their errands, sleeping on the floor, and eating at the second table on their account, is to exaggerate the feelings I entertained in those days.

Ministers' sons who were so short-sighted as to be born a generation ago did not always look forward to the Sabbath with enthusiasm. If the few who have survived the perils of their early lives could speak, they would say that they were surfeited with meetings. The weekly lesson must be drilled into us at the home end of the line, and drilled out of us at the Sunday-school end of it. The innocent amusements that enlivened the exercises for the other boys we could enjoy only by stealth, by reason of the liability of being called to account for it then and there by the paternal pastor on the platform.

Then the preaching services meant more for the parson's sons than for the other boys, for while the average boy could solace himself with his library book during the closing exhortations, such arrangements were not permitted to the clerical scions. When I used to read in those old slavery days of the horrors of the middle passage, I imagined they were something like the horrors of the front pew. This seat was always reserved in New England for the minister's family; or, to be more accurate, the minister's family was reserved for it. It was purely a New England device, and I have always laid it up against the Pilgrims. No one would hire the pew; and if all else forgot, the preacher's family should remember that life was a vale of tears. The front pew would do the business. Looking back upon it, I still consider that as a seat for boys, it is the best evidence of " man's inhumanity to man." There is no place for the growing feet of a growing boy; there is no scenery but the minister and the pulpit; all the other boys are behind; if the minister wishes a glass of water, the front-pew boy is the one that the beckoning finger lights on first. Then the angle of vision is severely acute; the head must be thrown back if one would be diligent to see how many more pages before the amen; the neck aches severely, although as the minister's son is supposed to be ultimately hanged anyway, a little preliminary neck-stretching cannot much matter.

I was more than fortunate in the indulgence of my parents, and the ills I suffered were incident to my accidental birth as a minister's son. I used to suffer in the matter of clothes; not that I did not have enough, — the trouble was I had too many. It happened in this wise. On Mondays the preachers met in Boston. The ready-made clothes movement was just starting, and Oak Hall led the craze. Here, on their way to the cars, the preachers would stop after taking their theology at Cornhill. Now, one cannot always carry a parson's boy in his eye; and with the uncertainty of all guessing, and the natural parental inclination to allow for growth, my Oak Hall clothes seldom used to fit me till the patches began to come, — there being such a general bagginess about the trousers that I found myself in the condition of the other boy who could seldom tell whether he was going to school or coming home.

It was a good thing for the poor, but not so fortunate for me, that my father was a preacher of practical charity. When we moved out of the then narrow, ready-made clothing zone, I was the involuntary victim of impoverished tailors, who were employed by the kind-hearted minister because no one else would give them work. I don't think that even in the last threadbare stages, the clothes ever got rid of the smell of the tobacco and gin which solaced their creators; and though I was not naturally an uncomely youth, it would be distorting history to say that I was "the glass of fashion and the mould of form."

I am not undergoing an examination for ordination,

and therefore may seem to be going out of my way in saying that I was called to the pulpit when only eight years of age. It came about in this way. I was sitting in one of the side seats with a neighbor's boy. We were negotiating a transfer of knives, and were a little at loggerheads as to the amount of "boot." I have no doubt we were somewhat animated, for we both had a turn for business; at any rate, the preacher suddenly stopped, called my name, and did not exactly invite me into the pulpit, but said in a kind of peremptory manner that I would come up at once.

Of course there was no reason why the other boy should not have come too; if he had, I should not have cared, for we could have finished the trade. But no, he was not a minister's son, and could swap knives with the whole congregation with impunity. Eighteen years after that, I went into the same pulpit and preached; but all through the service I could not help wondering where the other boy was, and what became of the knife I lost.

On the whole, then, the minister's son has some trials in fairly getting launched into the world. He has, on the other hand, very many peculiar blessings, which perhaps may excuse us from any great expenditure of sympathy for him. While taught by precept and example the ways of peace, he does not as a rule bear so heavily the responsibility of his father's office that he will not take a hand in his own defence if the impositions crowd unpleasantly; and as a rule, we think his good conduct is at least as good as the run of boys. The youngsters of whom we have written were the boys of thirty years ago, and are now jogging along into middle life. Very many of them, despite the hardships of their youth, have taken up their father's profession, which proves that manhood forgets boyhood's trials, and that the old theory that one avoids the fire that burned him, is not always true.

AN ALASKAN VOYAGE.

THE voyage to Alaska is without a parallel in grandeur and variety of scenery. From Vancouver to Sitka, the course is through land-locked channels from one half a mile to three miles in width. Great mountains are on each side, many of them snow-covered; and from the channel, bays extend far into the land lined with pleasant shores. The mountains are forest-covered, the trees coming down to the water's edge.

There are few villages and no signs of life, except here and there a tiny fishing settlement, or the solitary canoe of some Indian fisherman. Wonderful fiords appear as the voyage lengthens; waterfalls drop their ribbon-like streams down the face of the mountains; delicious shadows lurk in the bays; mountains nine thousand feet high sentinel the way, while behind them, set against the sky, are great snow peaks. Only twice in the long voyage is the river-like passage open to the sea, and then only for a little distance. At times the Hudson River is suggested, occasionally the Rhine, often the Thousand Islands, very often the Danube at the place of its greatest glory, the Iron Gates. Farther north the round hills are like the Highlands of Scotland; in the northern latitudes for a little while, the islands are bleak, windswept, vegetationless like the Hebrides; but for all the distance, the scenery is incomparable in the beauty of quiet waters, the symmetry of hills and mountains, the serenity of sunlit bays, loveliness of inlet, sound, and river reaches, while the seaweed fringes the cleanest shores; and beyond, against the clouds, great Alpine peaks catch and hold the sunshine.

Alaska is nine times the size of New England, and as large as Great Britain, Prussia, Spain, and Italy. The western island of the Aleutian chain is only thirty-nine miles from Asia; and taking this as the western outpost of the United States, and Eastport as the eastern boundary, San Francisco is six hundred miles east of the centre of our country. Alaska is neither a State nor Territory; it is a reservation, like the District of Columbia, and is governed by the laws of Oregon. It has a population of thirty-one thousand, twenty-four thousand of whom are Indians. These Indians are a peculiar type, — Tsimpsians, Haidas, and Tlinkits. They have a common language called Chinook, a kind of patois devised by the Hudson Bay Company for commercial uses. Its vocabulary does not consist of more than three hundred words, although with its mnemonic qualities it is capable of a wide range of expression. The language has no literature nor grammar, and is intermixed with the dialects of the different tribes. The natives are unattractive, small in stature, in the north weak-limbed from life in their canoes, faces broad and expressionless, — a coarser type of the Japanese, without any of the lithe, sinewy movement that belongs to the Eastern tribes. Previous to the coming of the missionaries they were very degraded. Even now their manner of living is barbaric. Their homes are huts, and their meals are eaten from the floor.

The vegetation of Alaska is luxuriant. Sitka is fifteen degrees north of Portland, and though the Alaskan voyage takes one as far north as the latitude of Greenland, yet the isothermal line is that of the District of Columbia or Devonshire, England. Only four times in thirty-six years has the thermometer reached zero. A warm Japan current, called the kurosiwo, touches the coast, and makes a luxuriant vegetation. The ferns are almost man-high, and the tangles suggest those which Stanley found in the heart of the dark continent. There is great moisture, and the heavy precipitation gives the mountains their shining crowns, feeds the glaciers, forces vegetations, brings every leaf and twig to its fullest perfection, and keeps the foliage so fresh and dewy that at times the green almost dazzles with its intensity. Day after day the voyage goes on, through great river-like reaches, by majestic scenery, shimmering waters, gleaming cascades, rounded islands. There are glimpses of sounds opening into other sounds, waterfalls trailing their feathery mists over the face of cliffs, mighty bastion-like mountains glistening with the waters of melting snows or scarred with the trail of old avalanches.

Not until the borders of Alaska are reached, is there any town of fair population. Fort Simpson is almost on the boundary line. It is a northern Nantucket in the quaint beauty of its situation. The water is as clear as crystal; the tawny rocks and ledges are shell-covered, hung with draperies of seaweed; tiny roads skirt the village; there are curious totems carved with every fantastic figure, and the village is thrifty and attractive. Fort Wrangel, Sitka, and Junneau are the principal towns of Alaska. The first is a decayed village, which lost its business when the mines in its vicinity were abandoned. Junneau is the largest town, and aspires to be a city. Sitka, the capital, is quaint in its architecture, with many memorials of the old days of Russian occupancy. It is beautiful for situation, has an imposing Greek church, the government buildings, and naval vessels in its harbor. There are remnants yet of the showy court that was once here, and not a few traditions of the gay life of Russian belles and officers who played here their little dramas of love and pleasure. The culmination of Alaskan scenery is at Muir Glacier. At the terminus of Glacier Bay, it lifts up its wall of ice three hundred feet. It is a mile wide, and with its lateral branches covers an area of three hundred and fifty miles. The vast moraines are deserts of desolation, while the sun changes into marvels of form and color the pinnacles and bastions of this great frozen wall. Travellers who have belted the world describe it as one of the earth's wonders; and a noted scientist says that in all his experience he recalls but two instances which affected him so powerfully as his visit here, — a sunrise on the Himalayan range and the view of the midnight sun from the North Cape. Everywhere on the Alaskan voyage one is impressed with the vastness with which Nature has done her work. Many of the islands are as large as States. Nameless mountains have Alpine heights; glaciers which would excite wonder elsewhere are as yet unchristened; bays in which great ships could ride are unexplored, and inlets fair as a vision have no habitation. For hours the voyager passes through channels which excel the Rhine in beauty; through bays which in the blueness of their waters, the glory of their mountains, the intensity of their colors, suggest the Bay of Naples; and yet he must look upon the captain's chart to find the name of the wonder places.

The voyage is long, but the sight of Mount Fairweather would compensate one for the journey were there no other attractions along the way. It is sharply defined against the sky, shapely, massive, and yet delicately lined and superbly draperied with snow. Other mountains obtrude their black anatomies and crease the ermine mantle which covers them; but this queen of mountains shows no rent nor crease in the splendid robes she wears.

The sky is blue above and beyond, and the sunlight illumines the snow and changes it into something ethereal. Every moment the vision changes, but only to take on new grace. The clouds seem to be attendant courtiers, and the sky the background for the spectacle; while the mountain with gentle coquetries, as if conscious of her beauty, changes form and hue, attitude and pose, as if she knows that she is holding hearts and eyes captive with her witcheries. The mountain does not overawe with mere bulkiness; it does not appall with its magnificent height, although it can look down upon Mont Blanc; it fascinates by the grace of its proportions, and woos by the gentle ministries of its almost human graces. The great glaciers awe one by revealing human weakness: they appall with the sense of resistless power, and awe by the vast mysteries of force and time; but it is only the terror of fear that is awakened, and one comes away from them with stilled hearts, as if seeing the workings of resistless fate. But this mountain gives a sense of comradeship. Its messages are tidings of beneficence. It feeds the streams which run among the hills; it holds the clouds captive, and changes them to miracles of mercy, and marries strength and beauty in the strength of the hills and the grace of its sunlit snows. The voyager, when the journey is over, has memories of great ranges snow-covered, islands that were like emeralds set in azure, channels that were rivers, bays that were like lakes, great glaciers which held wonder dumb, and sunlit peaks which gave to speech the language of rapture. But, queen and monarch of them all, abides the royal peak of Fairweather draperied with the snow and jewelled with the sun. What the cathedral of Milan is in one's memories of Europe, peerless and unrivalled, that is Fairweather among the deathless remembrances of an Alaskan voyage.

The unique feature of Alaska is the totem. The totems are great trunks of trees or poles carved into the grotesque images of animals, fishes, birds, and all monstrosities. They are not religious symbols, but are the coats-of-arms of families, heraldic devices, the art the rudest, but giving in symbol language the traditions of their race. The tribes trace their origin to the animals or birds that surmount these

totem poles, — the raven, bear, whale, or seal. There is a folk-lore which runs through all the northern tribes. A raven was their ancestor. He made a man and locked him in a kind of Pandora's box; but he escaped and made the moon, and the moon made all the peoples, and they made all the troubles of the world. In the old days these totems were the heraldic signs of great chiefs, raised with curious ceremonies, the memorials of traditions the very memory of which has now passed away. How strangely life preserves its past, and how every people tries, in its own rude fashion, to make the symbols of its dreams and visions! Greece writes them in her Homeric songs. Rome carves the figure of the wolf that suckled the fabled founders of the city. The Northmen still sing the sagas of their Viking kings; while that deep instinct of humanity which makes wiser people keep their traditions, bids this ruder people keep the memorials of their fabled past, and so, following the world, —

> "They painted on the grave-posts
> On the graves yet unforgotten,
> Each his own ancestral totem,
> Each the symbol of his household,
> Figures of the bear and reindeer,
> Of the turtle, crane, and beaver."

THE STOCKING AT THE CHIMNEY.

I HAVE never been reconciled to the Christmas Tree. It is very beautiful, with the brilliant lights flashing against the dark aromatic branches, and there is something in its fragrant greenness that makes it a fit symbol of the Christmas festival; but when its branches bear our gifts it is a usurper, and not a friend. It was made to be a thing of beauty, not a beast of burden; its fruit is fragrance and greenness, telling us that as its beauty exists in the midst of winter's desolation, so Christmas Day stands green and fragrant amid the sorrows and woes of a wintry life. We cannot tie the fruits on alien trees, nor can we with our strings and pins make our Christmas Trees easily bear other fruit than that which they distil from their inner juices.

I do not wish, with any little pessimisms, to dim a single light that glows amid the Christmas branches; but to accept without protest the Christmas Tree as the messenger of our gifts is to be disloyal to the old Stocking at the Chimney, — which is one of the brightest memories of childhood; and as life lengthens, the mind becomes tenacious of its memories, and does not easily see the old loves and associations displaced by new customs.

Why, the very stocking that we used to hang, had meaning. Night after night the patient mother fingers had knit the stitches by the fireside or the evening lamp; we had held the tangled skein out of which, with loving patience, it had come; and the foot that wore it could feel the very warmth of the mother heart and the tender caressings of the mother hand that had made it. There is a finer grace and larger beauty in the " hose " we buy, — a smoother finish, woven of finer threads; but somehow our fine machines lack the mother touch that thrilled from the fingers into the old knitting-needles, and deposited in their weavings the sympathy and love of motherhood. No, the machines of our inventors never can make such fabrics for our wearing as the tired hands of our patient mothers made, so long ago.

Then the hanging of them by the chimney-side! Why, for days and weeks we had chosen the very spot where they should hang, with their open mouths set against the chimney, lest, after all, it might be true that the good saint who loved the children did come down the sooty way, and might in all the calls he had to make before the morning somehow overlook us, unless we made easy way for the presentation of his gifts.

Some of us never have regretted much that we were born so late, except when we have seen in some old houses the fireplaces of the long ago, and have heard the old folks tell of the good cheer that used to blos-

som at the open fire. There is a dreaming spirit that would have revelled in the lights and shadows of the old hearths; that would have seen a thousand pictures in the dancing flames, and have found congenial friendships in the spirits of the woods set free by the emancipating flames. We have the open hearth with our modern homes. It has not amplitudes of hospitable space, nor is it dark with great sooty background painted by a thousand fires; but it is a hearth on which the ashes fall as gray and soft as ever ashes fell; the brasses that hold the wood reflect our faces; the smoke goes up in fleecy plumes; in the flames we can see the pictures; and before the fire we can sit and dream, and build our castles, — not so high nor vast as once we reared them, but still grand and beautiful; and in the background, behind the smoke and flame where the field of vision is, even now we can see the white sails of our ships sailing homeward to this very hearth, bringing from far Cathay the very treasures for which we have been waiting, oh, so long! But it is not the old hearth where the crane hung, around which gathered the domestic and the social divinities, every brick saturated with the good cheer of a thousand feasts, by whose fire the food of generations had been prepared; by whose flame children had studied their lessons, and age had entertained its memories.

We believe, of course, that the world is getting better; that "the thoughts of men are widened with the process of the suns;" that "Time's noblest offspring is its last;" that we are in "the foremost files of time;" that "the old order changeth ever for the new;" and all that sort of thing. But it is useless for any one to tell us, especially while we are in this reminiscent mood, that the world can be quite so good and noble beside a base-burner as beside the open fire upon the hearth. We would not at any other time confess how great pagans we yet are, although we have always lived among fairly Christian people; but the old mythologies are not converted out of us. We know that there are spirits in the woods, for we have often heard the rustling of their wings; there are nymphs that haunt the streams, for we have seen their footprints; and there are fireside spirits that haunt the flames, and come down our chimneys and look at us, and then bear away the messages of those that trust them. We should all be sorry to have these gentle divinities go out of our life. But just think of our entertaining them at an airtight stove; think of holding converse with the invisible spirits of the air beside a steam radiator, or sending one's dreams through the meshes of a japanned register. One wishes, when the winter night is on, and the snow blows, and the house is still, to dream awhile, to let fancy paint its pictures, imagination rear its castles, memory call up the touch of vanished hands and the music that has died to silence in our dumb hearts. Out of the ashes of the open fire come the shadows of the past; in the flames the dreams are pictured every one; and we know, what we have long guessed, that dreamland is as real as earth itself. But think of holding our communion by a nickel-plated stove, whose flames are sullen because the ashes clog the grate; whose odors are very gassy unless the damper has right adjustment; or worse than this, if one would meditate, he takes his chair and draws up to a hole within the wall, being obliged before he can even feel the radiance of heat to go into his cellar and rake the clinkers out, and set the automatic damper, — to turn on the dreams, as it were, by filling up the boilers and letting out the cold air from the pipes. No, Count Rumford meant well, of course; but when he invented stoves, he put off the coming of the kingdom, and made it harder to christianize the world.

Of course I am often asked if I believe in Santa Claus. Well, I am not telling all my heresies or superstitions, and will wait until some larger heretics are settled with before I go into the confessional; I will only give one fact from my own experience, and leave it to the sceptics to explain. There used to live within my home a tiny girl. She has long since exchanged herself for another and larger one, not so large as she hoped to be, but twice as big as we wish she were. Well, before a certain Christmas Day that came when she was small, and we were young, she made a list of all the things she wished. Through all the autumn she worked upon it, correcting and revising, the process, however, consisting always in additions rather than elisions; and when the list was finished every item bore the prophecy of bankruptcy to us. She naïvely asked us, as we scanned the schedules, if we thought that Santa Claus would rise to the occasion. She half believed the heresy that the only Santa Claus there is, lives at the lower end of the chimney, but she was not sure. She knew that he was either at the top or bottom of it; and she thought that between us both we somehow could arrange it. Well, we told her to write her orders out in good clear hand, such as an old gentleman in the dark could read; to put it within an envelope, direct it to Santa Claus, put it up a chimney some days before, then hang her stocking near by, go to bed on Christmas Eve, and wait results. And she did it just that way, sending supplementary messages from time to time by the same post, with special instructions as to the things that should not be omitted if the order was to suffer any amendment. Well, on Christmas Eve the register was taken out, and the letters were gone, showing that Santa Claus must have received them; and on Christmas morning there she found in the very spot and in the very manner of her instructions to Santa Claus the very things for which she had asked. If this does not prove that there is a Santa Claus, why, we should like to know just what kind of proof would satisfy the unbelievers.

It is all very well, this having the Christmas Tree in the afternoon or evening, with well-mannered children, dressed in flounces and "patent leathers," sitting decorously on fine-spun carpets with the caterer's pans and cans in the kitchen for the Christmas feast, and kind-hearted parents, who have been coaxed and bullied into buying presents, sitting by, every child knowing that the boxes on the trees contain the very things that he has personally selected, and if not, he must know the reason why, and every parent knowing that if there is one thing omitted, explanations will be in order. Oh, this Christmas business in evening dress, with hired orchestra and refreshment *à la mode*, is dreadfully "swell," as the saying is; but it is a great bore, and a fearful fraud upon both children and parents.

Why, the planning and the surprising, the whispered consultations, the wondering curiosity, the feverish anxiety, the expectations and the fears, are half the joy of Christmas. The smuggling into the house of clandestine goods, the hidings in drawers and closets and attics, the little fictions of hard times and lean purses, the simulated indifference to appeals and suggestions and hints that are more than hints, the refusing face and the assenting heart, the little denials and the large sacrifices, the repetition of the old miracle of how the cruse of oil shall be used and not spent, — there is nothing in life comparable to the sweet delights of these miseries. Why, we have seen mothers tired unto death with plottings and plannings for their children, and yet in the weariness there was the very ecstasy of love. We have seen parents robbing themselves of the necessaries of life, and feeling paid by the smile of the children's faces as they received the luxuries which were purchased at such costly sacrifice. And then the deliciousness of seeing the stockings filled; the wrappings and hidings; the loading of the precious freight into the argosies of love; the fitful and uneasy slumber of parents and children, whose couches are made sleepless by the angels of love and expectation that watch beside them; the faint glimmer of the morn; the timid cry out of the darkness, "Can I come?" the half-hearted pleading to wait a while that the children may have yet longer the luxury of anticipation and that the parents may enjoy the sweet comfort of love's sacrifices. And then when moments that have seemed like hours pass, and the pleading petition is repeated and assent is given, how like the springing of the torrent when the frost is broken, comes the pattering of children's feet, — a music sweeter than all the Christmas carols ever sung. The wonderment of it; the ecstasy of accomplished wishes; the finding of the very things anticipated, dreamed of, and yet every one of them wrapped around with glad surprises, as though they had never been heard or thought of before! The treasures of all the earth are here; and life, though it goes on for all the years and crowns itself with riches, and gathers art and every wonder that the world contains, shall never in older life have the zest, the thrill, the ecstasy, that comes when childhood is born anew on each Christmas morn, in the midst of the fragrant frankincense and myrrh, the holy gifts which love offers to its own.

The world is never so good again through all the year as on Christmas morning; for love then reaches the fulness of its tides, and then begins to ebb and ebb to the dreary flats of life's unloving work. As we grow old, the remembered thrill of the old home and its unselfish love comes back at times to reveal to us what childhood never saw, — that there is no love so patient and unselfish as the love of human homes. And as the children grow to manhood and womanhood how parents look back upon the earlier days and now interpret all the sacrifices that love made, and know at last that in them all there was the hiding of life's highest joy, and that it is true that life reaches its sweet flowering and fruitage in its self-denials.

There has come a vulgarizing of Christmas in later years. The demon ostentation has changed love's festival into a shopper's carnival, and made merchandise of affection. But the heart is undying in the instincts of its love; and though the fashions of pride and folly change, the old, old fashion of love survives forever. And by and by men and women will come back from the showy hypocrisies of life to the old hearthstone loves of home; and the stocking at the chimney, the heart love of parents and children, will reassert itself, and gifts will be once more measured, not by the skill lavished upon them by stranger hands, but by the love which gives to uncostly gifts a holiness all their own.

The Christmas gift of Christ was a gift of supreme, undying love! This is the meaning of it all: the Christmas songs sing love over the rejoicing world, the Christmas gifts are meaningless if they are not the dumb heart's speech of love; and the Christmas carol of " Peace on earth " is incomplete if it has not the glad refrain " Good-will to men," for peace can only come where love has lived.

THE LAST NIGHT IN THE OLD HOUSE.

WE are in a dismantled home. Every room is filled with memories, and to-night every remembrance is singing itself within our heart. To this home we came long years ago, and here the drama of the pleasant years has been enrolled; here friends have come; here there have been birth and joy, sunshine and music, laughter, mirth, the confidences of friendship, hours of toil, the vows of marriage, the weaving of the thousand threads of work and service that make the web of human lives. Everything but death. And every room has its history; and no palace of the Cæsars, however rich in historic things, has for us a tithe of the associations gathered around this pleasant home, within which to-night we sit for the last time, and from which to-morrow we go forth forever.

For more years than we dare to tell we have lived among our books within this study. It is not grand with carvings nor rich with relics of art; but we have dreamed many a pleasant dream within its walls, and have here spent delightful days and years. Kinder friends never sat within any home than have gathered here; and the books which, in spite of us, came one by one until they covered all the walls, have been silent but delightful companions, ready to

cheer us with their revelations or their silence, as our mood should be. And now they are all gone, taken from their familiar places and carried away, as though they were dead and had been sent forth for burial.

It almost seemed as if they too had learned to love the place where they had wrought their work; and hard as it was to send them away, it would have been harder still did we not know that on the morrow we shall follow them. We wonder if those who will live here when we are gone will see in the fire the old pictures that we have seen; if they will learn to love the vines which trail beneath these windows, and to have such pleasant friendships with the flowers and grasses of this little yard as we have had. We hope that the roses when they come will miss us just a little; and we think they will, for they always nodded to us, and turned their petals when they first opened to the window where we sat. We had no need to do it, and it was a waste of money and too impractical and foolish for us even to tell, except to friends who will not betray us; but after the deeds had passed, we had the old gardener come and set the vines in order after the winter's winds, and put the paths and beds in shape, that we might have, for the picture that memory will hold, the old yard with the order and beauty we had seen and loved for all the years.

These have not been easy days and nights for us. One does not know how deep run the rootlets of his life, nor how they twine with other roots, until he tries to pull them up for transplanting in other soils. We shall not try to tell the story of these days, which have been days of revelation to us, days when our hearts have been full of mingling tears and joy, — tears because it has been so hard to break our friendships, and joy that we had friendships which were hard to break.

And yet if only our readers will forget that we are

speaking of ourselves, and remember that we are telling the story of every pastor who goes out to new fields, we may convey something that may be of service to us, whether we are pastor or people. But whether it shall serve or not, we can write of nothing else on this last night, when we sit down by the old fire within the old room which to-morrow will have an alien tenant.

It is the fashion for men to think that the pastor's life is one of hardship; that it is thick with cares and busy with unrequited toils: that it offers no prizes for ambition, and has no rewards for devoted effort. Education and refinement, which are the essential equipments of ministerial success, create taste and appreciation for the luxuries of life, and yet the ministry is without the wealth which brings these things. Desiring art and the costly instruments of cultured life, the daily toil brings only subsistence, while the future calls up an apprehension of the poverty so galling to the pride and independence which cultivated self-respect has created. It is not often that fathers choose the ministry for their sons; and even the mother heart, which is so true and loyal in its love, which desires for its children not greatness but goodness, not wealth but honor, only with a pang sees its offspring select the ministry for its life-work. Here and there is a pastor whose life has been hard and cheerless, who speaks of his work with regret, and cheats himself with visions of the prizes he might have won had he chosen differently, — so unwisely does the world see.

The ministry indeed is regarded as a field of effort with many labors and but few rewards. We can never remember the time when our life was not lived among the clergy. We were born in a pastor's home, and we have known the whole story of the preacher's work from our childhood's days. We have heard the tale of hardships and deprivations, have seen true and loyal men toiling in hard fields with scant rewards, frail wives and mothers growing prematurely old with burdens of hand and heart, and we are by no means ignorant of the shadow side of the profession to which we ourselves belong.

But with all this in view, we can think of no other field of effort so rich and certain in rewards as that of the ministry. What is it that men desire in wealth? Is it power? The preacher's office is a throne of power. Social rank? Education and character outrank wealth in every assembly. Is it entrance to circles of refinement? Every door swings on easy hinges at the preacher's approach. Is it opportunity of usefulness? Every field of helpfulness invites the preacher's aid and responds to his service; and if he has no wealth to give, he has the voice that can command wealth; and if his own arm is weak, he has the power to command the service of the multitudes, who are always ready for any leadership which is sincere and unselfish.

The splendid compensations of the ministry are revealed only to the few whose privilege it is to serve their people for many years. The ordinary pastorates terminate before these slow-growing tendrils of affection interbraid themselves with others; but when for long years pastor and people have lived together, severance brings a realization of all the compensations of those years. Ordinary fellowships are severed without pain; but friendships that are hallowed by the deep experiences of life become so interdependent that to separate them is to take away something of life. A pastor's life touches human existence as no other does. His words give inspiration; and we are always grateful to those who give us the thrill of higher ambitions and the ideals of nobler living. To every one who realizes the holy solemnity of marriage, three lives are bound together by its sacrament; for the hour of bridal, which is to woman life's supremest moment, makes an eternal picture in the mind, and in it stands forever the one whose words united two destinies in one. There is no soil that preserves the footprints of friends like that which is around an open grave; and no music of human speech is so undying as that which receives immortality of remembrance by association with the sound of falling clods. In all these great experiences of life — and they come at some time through the long years to every home — the pastor is associated; and when he goes out, it is for pastor and people the taking away of some of the foundation stones on which life is built.

A pastor's life is made up of service for others. The pastor is a public servant, and every cause and every individual seeks his help. His life is spent in making plans and devising aid for others, few thinking ever, as they draw upon his time and sympathies, that no one can give of his life to others except the "virtue" go out of him; and there is inevitable exhaustion. And so every pastor often asks himself, as he renders his unthanked services for others, "Will these labors which cost so much ever be appreciated by those for whom they are wrought?" And the years go on and the burdens multiply, until, when he is almost weighed to the ground with cares, and his life wearied with service, he learns, but never easily, to find in the ministry of service the reward of the toil that so exhausts the life.

Then some day the end comes, by death, perhaps; and when the eye that has so often been wet with tears for the sorrow of others can no longer see, the hands which laid unthinking burdens on the poor stilled heart weave loving flowers of remembrance into funeral wreaths.

Or perhaps the pastor goes to other fields, that he may find the rest which comes, not by idleness, but by change of work; and the revelation comes that his labor has not been in vain. He feels the tugging of a thousand heart-strings, and old memories that slumbered wake to life; voices that long ago died in the great silences speak again; every service finds a tongue, and every sacrifice comes back with blessings, and one has all the love and gratitude and friendship that death brings, without the pangs of dying.

So the little partition wall that separates the fountain of tears from the fountain of laughter is broken down by the surging of the waters, and sorrow and rejoicing intermingle at the pain of parting, — the joy being that friendship is so dear that the parting is made hard.

No joy that life brings is comparable to that of ministering to others' needs. This is not preaching nor sentiment, but the very philosophy of life. And there is no place in all the fields of human enterprise that is so rich in opportunities as that of the Christian ministry. No occupation is dowried with such splendid rewards; not rewards of gold and houses and the mere counters of material compensation, but the higher prizes of human love and gratitude, as much greater than the lower prizes of outward success as the purses of the modern race-course are inferior to the wreaths of olive-leaves which crowned the winners in Olympic games.

Do we bewail the fact that the young men are

not crowding the doors of our Theological Schools? Have we need for committees on the Increase of the Ministry? It is because the wondrous prizes of the ministry, its sweet rewards of friendship and love, are hidden in men's hearts as too precious things to be revealed to human gaze. It is because the world does not know how usurious is the compensation of the pastor, who is denied the common rewards of wealth that he may be enriched with the costlier payment of love and gratitude.

We are revealing no secrets of our merely personal life, or depicting that part of the picture of a pastor's life on which the sunshine rests, forgetting the shadow part. Our own life has been rich with unmerited kindnesses, abundant with undeserved blessings. We do not forget those who, with larger desert, have been set to toil in harder fields than those where our feet were set; but every pastor, wherever his lot and whatever his work, who has toiled long among the same people, will bear witness to the fidelity of our assurance, that the ministry is rich to affluence with the very highest compensations of life. Talk with old pastors who have given up their work and are in the world of business, and note the moistened eye, the tremor of regretful remembrance, as they speak of the joy of their ministry, and hear them tell that the days of their poverty were richer in all that makes life precious than are the days of their wealth. Yet the service that brings this triumph must be unselfish; men must give, hoping for nothing, remembering that they are set to minister, not to be ministered unto, and then the blessings will come, because they were unsought and unasked.

But the night is drifting on. While we are busy with these pleasant memories, which come back freighted with the fragrance of nearly a score of years, can it be possible that the years have taken away the spring of youth, that makes it look future-ward, not backward; or is it because this room, which grows dear as the hour of departure grows nearer, is filled with the invisible presences of the multitudes who have kept friendship's trysts with us before our study fire? How beautiful it is, as we confront new friends and work, to feel that the past, which has been wrought, is forever safe; that no failure of to-morrow can blot out the triumph of to-day; that the past enjoyments are secure, though to-morrow shall bring only disappointment; and that though one never shall find friends so patient to his faults as the old friends, the old friends, whether dead or living, are friends forever. And yet, thank God, the world is much the same whatever skies are over it, and for every one who tries to do his duty in humble but hearty fashion, the great world has ready its loving heart and its open hand. Love is the richest prize, and it is the easiest purchased: he who would have friends need only show himself friendly; and he who wants love can have it if only he will offer love in purchase.

So, somewhere in the world, there shall be another study fire; the new friends shall gather around it, and not one of the old friends shall we let go. Somewhere we shall find another study window, which will look out, we hope, upon the vines and flowers, and somewhere else we shall find friends as true and faithful as these whose remembered kindnesses are singing themselves to-night within our heart.

We shall not put any fuel to-night upon our fire, as has been our wont, for to-morrow we shall not come here to our daily task. The study fire will have gone out, and there will be only ashes in the familiar place. But nothing shall ever take away the pleasant friendships, the dreams and loves that have been witnessed here, nor rob us of the sweet delights that through nearly a score of years we have had within this pleasant room.

www.ingramcontent.com/pod-product-compliance
Lightning Source LLC
Chambersburg PA
CBHW021805230426
43669CB00008B/639